MW00990788

The C4 Process

The C4 Process:
Four Vital Steps to
Better Work

David Veech and
Parthi Damodaraswamy

Business Innovation Press
An imprint of Integrated Media Corporation
Louisville, Kentucky

Copyright © 2011 by David Veech & Parthi Damodaraswamy

All rights reserved. No part of this book may be reproduced in any form or by any electronic or mechanical means, including information storage and retrieval systems, without permission in writing from the publisher, except by a reviewer who may quote brief passages in a review.

For information, contact: **Business Innovation Press, an imprint of Integrated Media Corporation 12305 Westport Road, Louisville, KY 40245, 800-944-3995.**

Visit our Web site at http://store.kyalmanac.com/

First Edition: July 2011

Printed in the United States of America.
10 9 8 7 6 5 4 3 2 1

ISBN: 978-0-9832639-5-1

Designed by Kelly Elliott
Edited by Susan Owens

WHAT OUR READERS ARE SAYING

"*The C4 Process* is a must-read for leaders. Both the book and the method are clear and concise and should make it easy for organizations to rapidly improve their problem-solving skills. While creating a true learning organization requires everyone to participate, the C4 card makes problem solving accessible to everyone and, with leadership on board, should lead to proactive, not reactive, problem solving throughout the organization."

—Jason McVay, Senior Advisor, Compression Institute

"Work-group problem solving is easily and simply explained. Veech eliminates most excuses about not understanding what to do, but he points out more than once that the key is disciplined practice. It's like learning to play golf: not as easy as it looks and you have to keep in practice."

—Dr. Robert W. "Doc" Hall, author of *Compression: Meeting the Challenges of Sustainability Through Vigorous Learning Enterprises*

"*The C4 Process: Four Vital Steps to Better Work,* by David Veech and Parthi Damodaraswamy, is a very important book. For the past ten years, I have taught organizations the importance of empowering and asking people to participate in problem-solving activities. Magical things happen when you open the creativeness of workers. People get more excited about their jobs and the company improves its quality and productivity. While I would get people started, the C4 process takes an idea system to a much higher level. It gives workers many new tools to identify problems and to eliminate them. I congratulate the authors for putting together this fine new book."

—Norman Bodek, author of *How to Do Kaizen: A New Path to Innovation, and The Harada Method – The Spirit of Self-reliance*, and a member of *Industry Week's* Manufacturing Hall of Fame

"Problem solving is the key not only to your lean transformation but also to your competitive advantage and prosperity. It is important that you have a standard, common methodology and terminology that is simple to understand and implement for your entire organization. This book looks at problem solving in the 'big picture' as a process and not just a tool. It lays out this process as it connects to your company's vision, mission and strategy deployment (or hoshin), as well as to everyday 'floor tools' such as standardized work and Training Within Industry (TWI). This practical, hands-on guide, with many examples, case studies and tools, is a must-have for any lean practitioner."

—Mike Hoseus, former executive, Toyota Motor Manufacturing and coauthor with Dr. Jeffry Liker of *Toyota Culture: The Heart and Soul of the Toyota Way*

"I really enjoyed reading this book. While many ideas have been around for some time, I liked how David and Parthi captured the essence of problem solving and continuous improvement (CI) in a very comprehensive way. The simplicity of the C4 card and worksheet provide a very structured approach to problem solving and help foster a thorough understanding of CI project status. I cannot wait to try some of the new ideas I got from reading this book in my new projects."

—Alexander Pronin, Vice President, Continuous Improvement, Europe and Africa, Building Efficiency, Johnson Controls

"In *The C4 Process*, Veech and Damodaraswamy provide a foundational process from which people in organizations can build an effective learning environment. This type of environment is essential to building a lean enterprise and creating a culture where people have the skills to truly solve problems of any scale effectively. The C4 process is a proven means of resolving problems through people, and this book illustrates the details and actual examples of how to apply it successfully. It is a must-read for anyone truly interested in developing people to transform an organization."

—**Jim Huntzinger, president and founder of Lean Frontiers**

"David Veech and Parthi Damodaraswamy have done a remarkable job of presenting a clear and practical approach to problem solving. For many organizations, the reporting system offered by the C4 cards alone would be an improvement, but the book's philosophy of Concern, Cause, Countermeasure and Confirm goes much deeper. By teaching the difference between identifying core problems and solving them, versus simply complaining, *The C4 Process* gives teams the vital tools they need to achieve transformation in the workplace."

—**Barbara Jean Walsh, Education Manager,**
***Professional BoatBuilder* magazine, Brooklin, Maine**

"One of my favorite books of the early 1990s was *Management Mistakes and Successes*, by Robert F. Hartley. In it, he shares the 3 C's: conservatism, conceit and complacency. These core attitudes can render any organization a victim to its competitors. Now seasoned professionals David Veech and Parthi Damodaraswamy present *The C4 Process: Four Vital Steps to Better Work*. The four C's in this seminal work—Concern, Cause, Countermeasure and Confirm—are the perfect answer to the negative attitudes that threaten organizational longevity. *The C4 Process* is a pragmatic approach to driving sustained, positive change and innovation in an organizational setting. Content that is easy to read and apply, complemented by excellent tools, make this book *the* manual for implementing continuous improvement throughout an organization. I recommend it highly."

—**Robert C. Thames, author with Douglas W. Webster of**
Chasing Change: Building Organizational Capacity in a Turbulent Environment

For my mom, who taught me to aim high and that there weren't any limits to what I could become; for my dad, who taught me the value of a solid day's work and the success that comes with it; and for my wife, Mary, and my children, Susie, Matthew and Danny, who give me the best reason to do it all.

David Veech

To my parents for the constant love, support and sacrifice that made me who I am today; to my uncle, Dr. Jayaram Lingamanaicker, who inspired me to set high goals and then helped me fulfill them; and to my wife, Sathya, and daughter, Abbhi, for their sacrifice and enduring support.

Parthi Damodaraswamy

Table of Contents

ACKNOWLEDGMENTS

This book is the product of many years of teaching, testing, learning and listening to hundreds of friends, clients, supporters and partners. I am grateful to them all, but there are a few I need to call out clearly.

Mike Kirkby from Rolls-Royce was the one who started me thinking about C4 in earnest. I'd been playing with a new worksheet to offer a little more of a guide than the blank A3-sized sheet used elsewhere. Mike shared the Concern-Cause-Countermeasure action plan he'd put together and I adopted these words as block headings. Later I added Confirm because of the need to deliberately follow up.

Ray Littlefield, one of our partners at ILS, took the rough C4 form I'd created and started getting clients to provide feedback. Then, after we'd made some improvements, he rolled it out specifically as a requirement for all workshops we conducted in Australia. The feedback and projects from these clients, particularly from CRF, gave me valuable help in identifying our weaknesses in teaching the process, and what we learned made its way directly into this book.

Bill Duarte and Mike Lee from Columbia Forest Products (CFP) created the demand for the product and gave me a chance to experiment with it, particularly the C4 card. Brad Thompson and Dave Abts made sure that CFP rolled the C4 worksheet out to its mills and began using it enthusiastically. More great examples and more opportunities to learn flowed from this partnership.

Jason Oakley, Andrew Scott and Doug Clark of LINAK U.S. created a substantially modified C4 board to use with the C4 card, hoping to replace their kaizen suggestion system with the learning focus the card offers, though events beyond our control have prevented completion of this experiment in the immediate future.

Tim Paige at Libbey Glass gave me a copy of Dean Gano's book, *Apollo Root Cause Analysis*, to "give [me] something to think about." With input from this book and feedback from the many client groups who struggled with the fishbone diagram, I was driven to find a simpler technique to determine a root cause.

Brad Denning, Mike Shirley and Ryan Lewis of Skier's Choice spent a lot of time with me discussing their lean improvement activity sheets, which contributed to the development of the C4 card and the process to manage it.

Bill Stone and Tom Blades at Grote Industries asked some thought-provoking questions that drove me to rationally think through the purpose and the language of the C4. (Now if I can just get them to drop the C5 thing, we'll all be on the same sheet.)

Kim Huston, president of the Nelson County, Kentucky, Economic Development Council and author of *Small Town Sexy: The Allure of Living in Small Town America*, introduced us to Bobby Clark, our publisher.

Norman Bodek, president of PCS Press, introduced me to Quick and Easy Kaizen, which is designed to maximize employee participation in a company's transformation efforts. The simplicity of this approach was the standard I used for the C4 card.

Finally, the U.S. Army taught me how truly effective C4 can be, especially when packaged in a claymore mine and aimed properly. Here's hoping you, too, have "explosive" results from your use of the C4 process!

Introduction

Despite the ups and downs of global economies, the need for skilled or re-skilled workers has remained the difference between companies that thrive and those that struggle. The ability of an organization to continuously learn, innovate and change usually spells success and can put a firm at the top of its industry, profession or market. The best companiies build this capability internally rather than try to hire it or acquire other, more innovative businesses. To succeed they rely on the skill, ability and intellect of their entire workforce and have put in place critical structures and systems that reinforce the value their employees bring to the organization. In other words, they've created both better workplaces and better work.

Sadly, few companies recognize that developing skills in the workforce requires much more than having a robust training program. Just because a company offers 250 seminars and workshops doesn't mean it's a learning organization.

This book presents a tool leaders can use to drive effective skill development throughout their organizations. We call it C4. It focuses on creating better work and better workplaces by developing cognitive skills in people, teaching them how to solve problems at work by following a deliberate, step-by-step process. Implementing C4 requires leaders to change what they do so they can take on the role of coach for this process, and it dramatically turns away from the approach most organizations take to problems: letting someone else solve them.

Almost every day at one plywood manufacturing mill, the production superintendent noticed the output for the day fell short of what the plan required. There were hundreds of reasons why, and at the end of each day the superintendent required his supervisors to report these reasons. Every day the super got a stack of "5-why" cards from his supervisors listing the reasons they didn't hit their targets, reasons like "downtime on the pro-saw" and "two team members absent today" and "took 25 minutes to find the right core material." In short, supervisors provided five reasons why the problem wasn't their fault. Each day the super reviewed the cards, discussed them briefly with the leaders and handed them over to the "lean" guy, who stacked them on a shelf behind his desk. Each day the supervisors challenged each other not to let these kinds of things happen in the future. They kept happening anyway.

Each of us faces hundreds of problems every single day. What time do I have to wake up? What do I wear? What should I eat for breakfast? Where are my car keys? Most of the time, we solve these problems with little conscious thought. Our brains seem to be hardwired to solve problems, so when we have unsolved problems we're not happy. At work, unsolved problems can lead to frustration and dissatisfaction, which in turn can affect the quality of a company's product or service. As everyone knows, customer interaction with a dissatisfied employee can be distinctly unpleasant. Recent surveys have found that as many as 50 percent of professional workers report dissatisfaction with one or more aspects of their job. Figures are harder to find for hourly workers, but some suggest dissatisfaction for this group could be as high as 90 percent.[1] In the past dissatisfaction often showed up as absenteeism and turnover. This is less likely to happen today. Almost everyone has friends or neighbors who are struggling to find work, and many who have jobs are afraid of losing them. Nevertheless, the dissatisfaction is still there.

Unsolved problems may be the root source of almost all workplace dissatisfaction. Issues regarding pay and benefits, internal policies, promotions or growth opportunities and/or relationships with supervisors reflect problems that haven't been properly solved, and most unsolved problems point to leadership. We just aren't developing our leaders to solve problems effectively. That's where this book can help. The C4 process is for everyone in the organization. First, leaders learn the process; then they teach it, which forces them to interact and build relationships with the workforce. And it is this collaboration, using a common set of tools understood by all, that allows an organization to solve problems in a way that finally works.

Because human beings possess a natural problem-solving ability, we have a tendency to shortchange the role of analysis when problems get sticky, which is exactly why we need a structured approach. Without structure we end up jumping to conclusions about what the problem really is, skipping the part about what's causing the problem, and rushing in to "fix" the problem as quickly as possible. Of course, some of these quick solutions may work for a while, but most fail over time. It's easy to get caught in a cycle of trial and error.

1 http://newsroom.accenture.com/article_display.cfm?article_id=5163, March 4, 2011.

The flowchart shown below, which has been circulating on the Internet for years, represents a typical approach to problem solving for far too many companies.

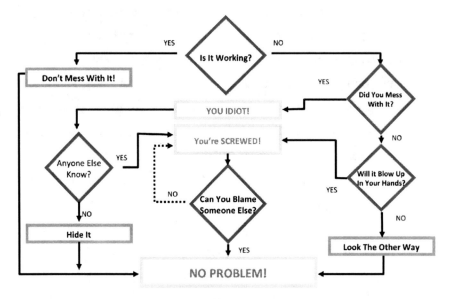

While we aren't always explicit in saying "you idiot" or "you're screwed," we do spend much of our time hiding problems we may have caused, ignoring problems that won't have much of an impact on us personally or finding others to blame. None of these approaches solves the problem.

Few organizations have a single, well-defined problem-solving process. More often, they have a select group everyone thinks of as the "problem solvers." These folks could be members of the quality or engineering departments or perhaps part of a continuous-improvement team. Most of the time they receive very good training, but the organizations they work for fail to recognize the importance of involving *all* employees in identifying and solving workplace problems.

In contrast, the C4 process involves everyone by reframing an organization's problem-solving approach from one of *reactive* response to one of *proactive* skill building. If a company can turn on this problem-solving ability in every employee, it's sure to identify many more problems—a quick look at the flowchart above illustrates why—but as quickly as these problems are identified they'll be analyzed and solved. *And this time they won't come back!*

CHAPTER 1

C4 Overview

Any time something happens that we don't expect, we have a problem. Our expectations may be explicit, perhaps a work requirement, or implicit, something we know from personal experience. In either case we weigh our current performance against our expectations; if there's a gap, we have a problem. Sometimes the problem is obvious, sometimes it isn't. And even when the problem is obvious, its causes can remain hidden. Sometimes we can solve a problem quickly; other times solutions are incredibly difficult to formulate.

There is no shortage of problem-solving processes. People have been studying this issue for years and countless articles and books have been written about it. Even what many view

> **Problem =
> Any time something
> happens that we
> don't expect**

as a relatively new problem-solving process (Six Sigma) is an evolution of Taguchi methods that have been in the works for over 50 years. What's missing seems to be _discipline_ (the stick-to-it kind, not the punishment kind). Often succumbing to time pressures, we too readily abandon any structured approach we might know in favor of our gut feelings, which leads to poor analysis, poor synthesis, poor evaluation and poor execution.

We also have a tendency, particularly in Western cultures, to elevate problem solvers to heroic status. We like heroes. People who can swoop in and solve a problem are usually the first to be noticed by senior leaders or the masses and are rewarded with upward mobility or thrust into leadership roles within their organizations. This cycle of cause and effect convinces everyone else that solving problems is not their job. Even worse, because there are often severe consequences for problems—like failing to lock out a machine when doing minor maintenance—workers learn it's often better not to report any problem they can't handle themselves and hope nobody discovers it before it's impossible to trace back to them.

Organizations with controlling structures and controlling leaders often discipline (the punishment kind, not the stick-to-it kind) those closest to the problem, even when these people may have no control over the course of events. This behavior is particularly troublesome. Not only does it lead to a culture of blaming others, it also fails to solve the problem. If all the energy put into hiding problems, avoiding problems or blaming someone else for problems were put to work actually *solving* problems, how much better could we make our organizations?

Changing an ineffective blaming culture to a successful problem-solving culture requires a new way to look at problems. And that's where C4 comes in. The C4 approach employs a standard process everyone can understand and teach to each other while simultaneously solving problems. Keep in mind, however, that even the best structure requires disciplined leadership to enforce the standard and guarantee learning.

Most problem-solving methodologies seem to have evolved from the cycle first introduced by Walter Shewhart in the 1930s and known as

Plan-Do-Check-Act or PDCA. W. Edwards Deming, a Shewhart protégé, re-emphasized PDCA in his teachings in Japan in the 1950s, though his focus was on the *Check* stage. He went so far as to relabel this stage *Study*. Deming urged organizations to put systems in place to study the outcome of processes and then to make adjustments to those processes based on what they learned (*Act*). The image below reflects this cycle as a continuous-improvement strategy. The incline reflects performance, the triangle reflects the standard to prevent backsliding, and the arrow reflects a drive to keep pushing to make the process better.

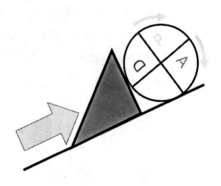

One of the biggest challenges with PDCA is in the *Plan* stage. Without specific learning and practice, it's difficult to understand what type of planning leads to effective problem resolution. Typically, organizations rely on tribal knowledge to take action whenever they detect a problem. One "expert" claims awareness and understanding of the problem and imposes a solution. When the solution fails to eliminate the problem, the organization tries something else in an ongoing stream of trial and error. The process quickly becomes a seesaw of *Do*-then-*Act*, *Do*-then-*Act*. The *Plan* and *Check* parts of this process are abandoned completely.

The C4 problem-solving process describes the steps a little more clearly than Plan-Do-Check-Act. It also incorporates some of the newer thinking of A3 problem solving used by lean companies, as well as elements of Six Sigma's DMAIC process (Define, Measure, Analyze, Improve, Control), and even some features of TRIZ (the Theory of Inventive Problem Solving).

C4 is simple enough that everyone in the organization can use it for problems big and small and easy enough that leaders can teach it to others. Moreover, it's non-threatening, maybe even a bit fun.

C4 breaks down problem solving into four key activities, each starting with the letter "C." Following these four steps—*Concern, Cause, Countermeasure* and *Confirm*—enhances people's ability to think critically and thus to diagnose and solve problems. In short, C4 provides an organization with the foundation for its *learning system.*

Here's how the process works:

- Step one clearly states the *Concern.* In other words, "What's the specific problem we need to solve?"
- Step two finds the root *Cause* of the problem, recognizing there's likely to be more than one root cause.
- Step three develops one or more *Countermeasures* to eliminate the root cause(s).
- Step four *Confirms* that the countermeasure(s) solved the problem for good.

C4 is an iterative process. The *Concern* stage begins by recognizing the symptoms of a problem and then exploring all potential problems that could manifest those symptoms (think medical diagnosis). From this potentially very large list, the next step is to identify the data required to analyze these potential

Concern
1. Understand the current situation.
2. State the symptoms, identify the "real" problem and set a new target.

Cause
3. Find the root cause(s).

Countermeasure
4. Formulate and evaluate alternative solutions (countermeasures).
5. Plan and implement selected countermeasure(s).

Confirm
6. Standardize and teach the improved process.
7. Track results to ensure the solution is effective.
8. Update the standardized work for the improved process, then reflect on the experience and recommend improvements to the C4 process.

problems; collect, analyze, and organize that data; and then use the results of this analysis to identify the *real* problem.

Once the problem has been defined, the *Cause* stage repeats the process by broadly exploring all potential causes of the problem defined in step one. These potential causes are then examined in greater detail, eliminating or advancing them as appropriate until what is left is a very small set of the most likely *root causes*. Sometimes it's possible to pinpoint a single root cause; in the vast majority of cases, however, there will be some interaction of root factors that becomes the root cause.

Only after that small set of root causes has been identified is it possible to develop one or more *Countermeasures* to eliminate them and thus resolve the problem. Developing such countermeasures employs the same strategy used in the previous two steps: Broadly explore all ideas for potential solutions to the problem at the root-cause level and then—through experimentation, analysis and evaluation—select, plan and implement one or more countermeasures.

In some cases it's possible to know right away if the countermeasure(s) were successful. In many others it's necessary to monitor performance long enough to know if the problem has been solved. The *Confirm* stage forces follow-up and review of the results. It also requires study of a team or individual's execution of the process in a search for opportunities to improve future problem-solving efforts.

There are big, tough, wicked problems in the workplace, as well as small or routine ones. There are problems with a specific cause and problems with random causes. There are problems we react to and those we create deliberately for the good of the organization. (This might sound a little crazy, but setting a new standard as part of a continuous-improvement program creates a gap that problem solving closes.) Regardless of the type of problem or its origin, C4 can handle it.

Problem Solving versus Kaizen

A problem occurs when you have a target (either stated or implied) and you fail to hit it. Kaizen is a Japanese word that literally means "change for good," but usually translates as "continuous improvement." Continuous improvement requires that leaders challenge people to achieve new, higher standards. For example, if a worker has a target to pack six boxes per hour and she's consistently packing six or seven boxes an hour without any difficulties, a kaizen goal would be for her to pack nine boxes per hour (a 50-percent increase). In this case, the problem is defined as the performance gap between the six or seven boxes per hour the worker is able to pack using the current process and the goal of nine boxes per hour. Within the continuous-improvement process this gap is called the concern. The C4 process can be used to close it.

Most people wouldn't be able to achieve a 50-percent increase in productive output without deliberate changes to the processes and methods they use. We don't want people to work harder or work faster for kaizen; we want them to work better. When workers achieve a 50-percent increase in output but they feel as if their job is easier, they've experienced kaizen.

To help implement the C4 process, we've developed a couple of guides: the *C4 card* and the *C4 worksheet*, shown on the following pages.

The C4 card provides an abbreviated format suitable for small, daily challenges that can be fixed quickly but still requires the problem solver to think through the entire process. It's also a useful spot to record the improvement ideas people have every day, and it can work well as a suggestion form. We'll cover these uses in Chapter 7.

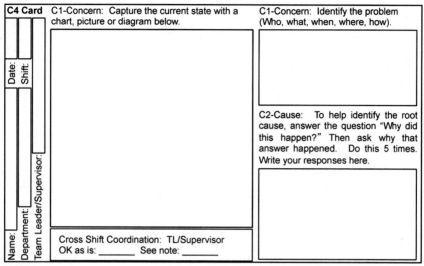

Front

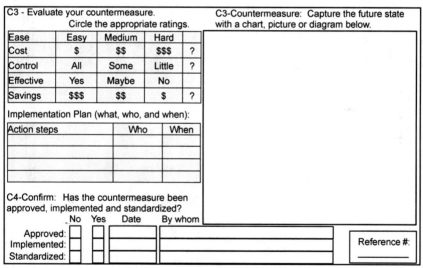

Back

Download this form to print and use in your organization at
http://www.clarkpublishing.com/forms/

For bigger, tougher, more complex problems, the C4 worksheet provides a structured sequence for teams to solve problems, keeping the team on track and serving as a document of record to preserve what's been learned. Teams addressing future problems should be able to access past

C-4 Worksheet
Concern – Cause – Countermeasure – Confirm

Theme: _____
Ultimate goal: _____
Date assigned: _____

Team Member: _____ Shift: _____
Team Leader: _____ Shift: _____
C-4 Coach: _____ Shift: _____

Concern: Understand the current situation
Use charts, diagrams, or photos whenever possible to describe the situation.

Who discovered the problem? Garner findings from any previous studies of the problem area.

Break down the larger problem. List the contributing problems below. Sorting them by category. Attach an affinity diagram.

Current State Value Stream or Process Map. Summarize here, and indicate where team can find fully detailed map.

Describe what is happening to indicate a problem.

Describe the ideal condition. What standard is involved if any?

When does this problem occur? How frequently?

What are the key problem areas on the map? (What are your angry clouds?)

What is this problem costing the organization?

Concern: Write your problem and goal statement
What do you want to accomplish? Be concise but as specific as possible. Make a statement of effect (OEE is consistently low – avg 46% when standard is 67%) and then tell an aggressive goal related to the Ultimate goal (Example: Decrease cycle time by 8 seconds by January) or a question to be answered (How do we get all team members trained on lean systems by the end of the year?).

Cause: Analysis
Brainstorm and organize potential causes or obstacles using the **Fishbone diagram, stem-and-leaf diagram,** or other organizing tool. Write the causes of the problem or obstacles to environment in the space provided always verifying that what you record is an actual CAUSE of the problem.

Priority Causes	What else?	Who else?	When?	Evaluation	Rank order

Cause: 5 Why Analysis
Problem

Why?

Why?

Why?

Why?

Why?

Therefore...

Statement of the root cause

Countermeasures
Brainstorm countermeasures and evaluate each potential solution, ranking them with 5 being best and 1 being worst. You may weight-load the categories according to company priorities.

Countermeasure	Cost	Ease to do	Control	Effectiveness (savings or performance)	Total

Selected Countermeasure (s):
Short Term:
Long Term:
Selection rationale:

Countermeasure: Implementation Plan
Develop an implementation schedule recording status and results as:
0 = Acceptable, Δ = Needs improvement, x = Poor

Implementation Steps	Who's responsible			Date complete

Confirm

Track Results
How long do we need to track results?
Number of req'd samples.
Method for tracking (visual?) and location of information.

Standardize
Date standardized work updated:
Document with before and after pictures for future training. Identify the location of these files for team members.

Reflect

People / Process / Teamwork / Results / Need for more training

©2010. ILS & David Veech. All rights reserved.

worksheets and supporting documents. Sometimes these records serve as a review of the process or a reminder of a particular technique or tool. Sometimes they simply offer a needed sanity check.

Teams and Quality Circles

The C4 worksheet can be pretty intimidating, especially for an individual. Let's say a worker observed a small problem or had an idea about how to make his work go a little quicker. Then suppose someone handed him a C4 worksheet and said, "Fill this out and we'll consider your idea." If the worker is like most people he'd quickly forget he mentioned it. "Never mind!"

With this in mind, we encourage organizations to put teams together to solve complex problems. To successfully complete a C4 worksheet teams need to work together. Organizations have always used teams to solve problems, but their effectiveness has varied widely. The best teams have a broad diversity of experience, are familiar with the theme or general problem area to which they're assigned, and have experienced some degree of team development. One type of team we encourage companies to establish is called a Quality Circle.

In 1967, Joseph Juran published a white paper[1] on a group problem-solving technique being used in Japan called QC Circles (for quality control). Juran recognized that the intent of Quality Circles was less about solving problems than it was about teaching teams how to work together, think critically and overcome individual fears.

This short paper was ignored until the 1980s, when Japanese products were dominating the U.S. market and U.S. companies were looking to exploit any Japanese management secret they could find. Unfortunately,

---

1   J. W. Juran, "The QC Circle Phenomenon." Industrial Quality Control 23 (No. 7, January 1967): 329–336 (available through www.ASQ.org).

Juran included in his report the claim that large Japanese companies using Quality Circles attributed about $10 million in annual savings to these activities. We say unfortunately, because that $10 million line is all most U.S. companies focused on.

Many leaders who heard about saving that much money from Quality Circles immediately mandated that every employee be part of a Quality Circle and that every Quality Circle solve x number of problems per month in order to generate that $10 million in savings. Quality Circles is a process-oriented concept, but U.S. companies trying to implement it focused almost completely on results. When the results didn't materialize, most firms abandoned the concept entirely.

Companies that applied Quality Circles as intended are still likely to be using them today. For example, over the past 20 years Toyota Motor Manufacturing, Kentucky, has maintained an average of 260 active Quality Circles at any given time. We suspect the company is realizing that $10 million savings each year but, more importantly, Quality Circle team members have learned how to solve problems, with or without formal Quality Circles.

In implementing the C4 process, one of the first hurdles a team needs to overcome is deciding to use the C4 card and C4 worksheet. The worksheet is particularly well suited for Quality Circle activities. It was inspired partly by Toyota's Quality Circles Theme Report, itself a highly prescriptive A3. Embedded in these guiding tools are a number of others, including:

- Brainstorming with a variety of techniques (see The Toolbox);
- Organizing and prioritizing tools like Pareto charts, check sheets, affinity diagrams and multi-voting;
- Analysis tools like cause-and-effect diagrams, stem-and-leaf diagrams, 5 whys and forcefield analysis;

- Decision-making tools like the decision matrix; and
- Planning and scheduling tools like Gantt charts and responsibility matrixes.

Not surprisingly, most people want to jump into solution mode as soon as they think they have a problem. What is surprising is how often people insist there's a serious problem when there really isn't. The C4 approach is designed to overcome both of these issues by supporting a different approach: stop, *think*, and proceed deliberately with a defined process.

C4 begins by examining the work being done, trying to gain an understanding of how it fits into the overall mission and vision of the company. The idea is to answer the question, "Why are we doing this?"

Slop and Magic

Sometimes the problem is obvious—a server crashes, an employee quits, an invoice doesn't get sent to a customer. If you ask any group of employees to brainstorm and list all the problems they can think of in a particular area (human resources policies, insurance claims processing, scheduling appointments at the dentist, and so forth), they could list hundreds. On the other hand, defining a *specific* problem for a group to solve, either as a Quality Circle, a kaizen team, a special projects team or a similar group, is more challenging than it seems. The process can be extremely frustrating and very sloppy. Whenever people restrain themselves from running with their gut reaction, they experience feelings of frustration. It's human nature to seek an immediate solution; we all want to find the magic.

The deliberate nature of the C4 process can feel like being stuck; like slogging through slop. And it's made even sloppier because activity occurs in the earliest stages of team development, when members are still trying to discover who amongst their teammates can perform. Without going through the slop, however, it's impossible to get to the magic. Every group the authors have worked with has experienced trial and error. They've all come into the process saying that it seems okay to redo something but not okay to take the time up front to do it right. Yet once they build in the discipline to stick with the C4 process, the amount of wasted time recovered is remarkable. The lesson is simple: Stick with the process, no matter how frustrating and sloppy it seems. In the end, those who do *always* get to the magic.

The Toolbox

BRAINSTORMING

As a problem-solving tool, brainstorming is both critically important and, at the same time, poorly understood. It's hard to imagine anyone reading this book who hasn't participated in an activity someone called brainstorming, not just once but several times. Typically, whenever a group of two or more people get together to discuss ideas or problems, we call it brainstorming. Even deciding where a group of coworkers should meet for lunch is brainstorming. (It's also problem solving, by the way.)

As applied within the C4 process, however, brainstorming has three specific requirements:

1. The group/team must be focused on a problem area.

2. The group/team must be made up of members with diverse backgrounds and experience.

3. Someone must record every concern, cause, idea, observation, etc., that the group/team generates.

There are two broad categories of brainstorming: *unstructured* and *structured*.

Unstructured brainstorming is what most of us have participated in for years: a group sitting or standing in a circle, throwing out observations or ideas while a "designated recorder" writes them down. Unstructured brainstorming can:

- Generate a large amount of information in a short period of time; and
- Generate energy in the group as people are able to build off each other's observations/ideas.

In addition, it's easy. Sometimes it's even fun. On the other hand, unstructured brainstorming:

- Makes it very easy to judge every comment in the group immediately, which risks alienating participants whose ideas are usually shut out;
- Often proceeds at a rapid pace, causing the scribe to paraphrase comments, an act which in itself is a form of judging the observations/ideas;
- Can lose the valuable input of naturally quiet or introverted people, who tend to withdraw as dominant participants take over; and
- Can sometimes get the entire group off track and focused on chasing irrelevant issues.

Structured brainstorming tries to overcome the negative aspects of unstructured brainstorming by adding controls to the process. Such controls are specifically designed to deal with the problem of more extroverted individuals dominating the activity at the expense of their less-vocal and/or less-assertive colleagues. For example, employing a technique where each person is asked in turn for input while other team members stay quiet gives each individual's input equal weight. Another approach asks team members to write their observations/ideas on small pieces of paper and hand them to the scribe, who then records them where everyone can see.

Our favorite structured brainstorming technique is called 6-3-3. Using this technique, participants are organized into groups of six. (A seventh person, someone outside the group, serves as facilitator and timekeeper.) Each person is given a blank sheet of paper. The facilitator then starts the time and everyone is given three minutes to write three observations or ideas. Participants focus silently on the problem area, recording their observations/problems/ideas in as much detail as they can.

At the end of three minutes, the facilitator asks each participant to pass his paper to the person on his right and then starts the clock again. Over the next three minutes, everyone reads the three items on the sheet he or she received and adds three more. The items they add must be different from what appears on the sheet and different from what they wrote previously.

This process continues at three-minute intervals until the sheets have been passed six times. At this point, each person should have the sheet he or she started with, with 18 recorded observations/problems/ideas. Given a field of six participants, the potential exists for 108 (6 sheets x 18 items each) identified problems or ideas, all gathered in under 20 minutes. Of course there will be duplication, making the actual number of real observations lower, but the group will still record significantly more items than during a typical unstructured brainstorming session.

The next step requires the group to organize this basketful of problems/ideas so it can take some action. For this we'll use the affinity technique described in detail in Chapter 3.

CHAPTER 2

The Foundation of an Organizational Learning System

O ne of the goals of C4 is to change the culture of organizations. Culture—the collective set of behaviors observed by people in the workplace—is the way things get done. Changing it means getting people to behave differently. A lot of people spend a lot of time wondering how to make this happen. Here's the bottom line: Until the organization starts doing something differently, the culture will never change. Implementing C4 fosters change by creating a new structure with a required set of new behaviors. If the rules of the new structure are enforced, over time the culture *will* change. If the rules aren't enforced, it won't.

At its core, problem solving is a cognitive skill we spend a lifetime developing. To set problem solving within the framework of cognitive development, let's refer to Benjamin Bloom's contribution to education.

In his *Taxonomy of Educational Objectives, Handbook 1: The Cognitive Domain*, Bloom describes how people learn through six levels: *knowledge, comprehension, application, analysis, synthesis* and *evaluation*.

At the first or *knowledge* level, we're able to recall information provided to us earlier by simply repeating what we've been told. Examples include the ability to recite safety rules or quote prices to customers from a published list. At the comprehension level we're able to rephrase what we've learned, describing it in our own words, and to explain the meaning of simple charts and graphs. At the application level we can use what we've learned in new situations. For example, after learning about a particular process or tool in a classroom, we can apply this knowledge to use the process or tool in the work area.

Most structured new-hire training programs take employees to the *application* level through a company orientation session and a basic introduction to the work they've been hired to do. If we stop there, however, if we're content with people who can only do what we've hired them to do, then we're not tapping the full potential that every employee brings to the workplace. If we use people *only* to lift or pull or assemble or make beds, we're simply substituting human power for machine power. Since the beginning of the industrial revolution human beings have become very skilled at automating processes, and in many workplaces around the world people are merely interchangeable pieces within those processes, just like cogs in a machine. But if we think of people as no more than interchangeable parts, we'll never get them engaged in improving the workplace and we'll be stuck with having specialists like engineers and managers solve every problem that occurs.

Knowledge
Comprehension
Application

Analysis
Synthesis
Evaluation

The three higher levels of learning, *analysis*, *synthesis* and *evaluation*, are problem-solving levels. Here we're able to take information from various sources, break it down into meaningful parts, and recognize the relationship of the parts to each other (*analysis*). We can then rearrange the parts and reassemble them into something different, add or remove parts or steps to add more value, or throw out the existing information altogether and create an entirely new process (*synthesis*). ⑤   ⑥

At the highest or *evaluation* level, we apply all of our previous experience to make a judgment about the value of something. This cycle of *analysis, synthesis* and *evaluation*, applied first to small, easily understood concepts or ideas and then to ever-more-difficult problems, builds a disciplined mind and gives people the confidence (or more specifically, the self-efficacy) to try new things, to experiment with their own work processes and to persist in the face of more difficult challenges. Imagine a workforce of several hundred highly skilled, highly competent, highly confident people identifying and solving the problems they encounter with great discipline. How could this type of organization fail in a competitive, global marketplace?

The C4 process provides a structure that requires people to work through the *analysis, synthesis* and *evaluation* levels of learning, thus building fundamental, cognitive skills within the workforce. This suite of skills includes critical thinking, quantitative and qualitative analysis, creativity, planning and organizing, evaluation, implementation and follow-up. Arguably, the most important of these skills is *critical thinking*.

CHAPTER 3

Concern: The Beginning of Critical Thinking

S tep one of the C4 process is *Concern*. In this step critical thinking forces us to clearly identify the problem we need to solve. Critical thinking is nothing more than deliberately asking and answering the following key questions:

Who? What? When? Where? How?

and then evaluating available evidence to determine the true nature of what is being observed. The *Concern* step explores questions such as:

- Who discovered the problem? (a far different question than *Whose fault is it?*)
- What happened or "What's the problem?"
- When did it happen?
- Where did it happen?
- How bad is it and how does it affect the organization?

One problem-solving team held a brainstorming session to identify key production problems. They settled on the problem of saw-damaged plywood panels coming out of the pro-saw. All team members agreed this was a serious problem that, if corrected, could save the company thousands of dollars a month. When the team collected and reviewed actual data, however, it discovered the problem occurred on only 0.31 percent of shop-grade panels (1,371 panels over a five-month period) and cost the company a total of $7,611 per year. The message is clear: Just because we think something is a problem, doesn't mean it really is.

When the team studied the impact of "out-of-square" panels instead, they found a more significant concern. In this case, the company produced on average 65 out-of-square panels per week (3,381 panels over the previous 52 weeks.) Out-of-square panels sold for an average of $22 less than on-grade square panels, so this problem had a potential savings impact of $74,382 annually. At the end of this and each subsequent chapter we'll use this example to summarize progression of the process through the four steps of Concern, Cause, Countermeasure and Confirm.

When confronted with a problem—remember, a "problem" is defined as any time something happens we didn't expect—it's often easy to see the symptoms but difficult to pinpoint the true problem. If we identify the wrong *Concern*, the true problem is very likely to return no matter how good the *Countermeasure*.

The C4 process uses critical thinking to build a series of tightening frames around the problem area. Each successive round of thinking brings us closer to the true *Concern*, the root *Cause*, or the right *Countermeasure* and keeps us from chasing irrelevant issues.

Someone's ability to see the truth is often constrained by his or her position in the organization. This same constraint can limit the scope of analysis. That's why the C4 process emphasizes a "go and see" approach (first defined by Toyota as *genchi genbutsu*). It's almost impossible to solve a problem without going to its source, or to where it was discovered, to see firsthand what happened. Analyzing what we see, and at what level, allows us to take responsibility for aspects of the solution we can implement personally and helps us to acknowledge when we need more help. Pulling a special team together to do high-level, critical analysis for routine, random types of problems is obviously not cost-effective. Conversely, an individual working alone, trying to solve a complex problem that affects a large part of the organization, has little chance of success. In fact, he or she could actually end up doing more harm than good.

Here's an example of a routine problem. Let's say a worker named Mary prints a document to a network printer. When she goes to pick it up she notices that, beginning on page three, the print gets lighter and lighter until by page nine the document is no longer readable. What's the *Concern*?

Most people would quickly conclude that the printer to which Mary sent the file is low on toner or ink. She can resend the document to another printer on the network, thus solving her readability problem, but if she does, the underlying problem—the printer is low on toner—remains for someone else to waste time discovering. Alternately, she can change the printer cartridge, run the diagnostics and reprint the document. Unless the document is still not clear (in which case there's a deeper issue), there's no need to tell the boss, call a meeting or assemble a Quality Circle. The problem has been solved.

It's important to stop at the *real Concern* to begin critical thinking. In other words, "What's happening to indicate a problem?" In this case the answer is not that the toner is low but that the document is unreadable. The *document* is the real problem, because that's how Mary *sees* the underlying problem. Framing the document as the concern ties directly to her work and its purpose, as well as giving her a customer-oriented reference point. An unreadable document clearly affects a customer, whether it's an internal customer (the boss) or an external customer. The low toner is a technical issue that could affect hundreds of customers, so it's critical to break down the larger problem and find its root *Cause*; otherwise, the problem will recur.

It's one thing to solve a relatively low-impact printing problem, but what if a long-term customer decides to buy from a competitor? What if a product coming out of the best operator's process unexpectedly fails an acceptance test? What if the employee turnover rate jumps to 21 percent when it's consistently been between 3 and 4 percent? What's the problem? Each of these examples clearly indicates a problem, but is it a problem that can be solved as easily as changing a toner cartridge?

Many workplace problems are small and can be counter-measured effectively with little effort. Still, it's important to track and document them. For one thing, tracking helps identify trends and patterns. For another, organizations can use these routine problems as opportunities to hone the critical thinking skills of their employees. One way to document small problems and teach critical thinking skills at the same time is to use the C4 card.

Both the C4 card and the C4 worksheet are vital tools for solving problems in the workplace. However, because the card represents an abbreviated version of the method, we'll start by reviewing the C4 worksheet. The worksheet is intended for use with a full range of concerns from the very simple to the very complex.

In teaching the C4 process, the authors have conducted more than 100 sessions of a lean systems course in problem solving, based on a hypothetical aircraft called the F3FV StrikeFighter (or StrikeFighter for short). Data collected during these simulations and from real-world examples help to illustrate the steps of the C4 process and show how these steps relate to the C4 worksheet.

The StrikeFighter System Simulation

The StrikeFighter simulation usually requires between 12 and 24 people to assemble 15 model-aircraft systems within a 30-minute production window. Each aircraft consists of 127 Lego® block pieces. Participants are divided into groups, each of which is responsible for a different major subassembly; one group is further responsible for integrating the completed subassemblies into the final aircraft for delivery to the customer.

Participants in the simulation normally work through three production rounds, responding to changing conditions in each round while learning the critical points of organizational transformation and improvement. Each group has 90 minutes to prepare for each round. The first round simulates a conventional, mass-production environment with discrete, functional departments that do limited types of work (usually driven by the color or shape of the Legos). Each group has a separate "warehouse" with all the pieces needed for its particular subassembly. Despite the availability of parts, however, a variety of structural constraints keeps most groups from delivering the required quantity of aircraft. At the end of the first round and before being introduced to the C4 process, each group identifies a list of problems experienced. After discussing the lessons learned, the groups prepare for round two.

During the second round participants have the same 15-aircraft requirement, but they are allowed to reorganize their assembly operations according to lean principles. The most significant change in this round is a requirement for supply-chain interaction. Each group no longer has all the pieces it needs to complete its particular subassembly in its warehouse. Every group has different pieces and parts, but none has enough to complete an entire subassembly. To illustrate the value of supply-chain interaction, each group becomes a supplier of specific parts to the general market; it sells parts to other groups so they can complete subassemblies and buys parts from other groups to complete its own. Each group must complete purchase orders and track parts shipments and receipts from the other groups. When the customer requests deviations from the standard aircraft, the groups must process change orders during the production run.

The complexity introduced in round two results in significant problems, problems that are often ill-defined. Groups then use the C4 process to identify and isolate key problems, conduct a root-*Cause* analysis and develop and evaluate *Countermeasures*.

During the third round of the simulation, the groups implement the *Countermeasures*. The third round brings no new re-quirements, but because the groups have climbed

Theme: Delivery - Delivered 4 StrikeFighters when 15 were due
Ultimate goal: Deliver 15 perfect StrikeFighters on time
Date assigned: 3/29/2011

Concern: Understand the current situation	Use charts, diagrams, or pho

In the upper left corner of the C4 Worksheet, record the theme, ultimate goal for this particular theme, and the date a team was assigned to solve this problem set.

the learning curve and solved the problems with a deliberate technique, par-ticipants always complete 15 aircraft in time periods ranging from 11 minutes, 30 seconds to 27 minutes, 14 seconds, based on a 14-minute target.

After the second round, the primary problem is clear: of the 15 aircraft required (the standard), only x were delivered. In this case, x represents an average of 4.5 aircraft. This is the *Concern*—the big picture, the big problem, the theme of this problem-solving activity. These same concerns occur in real organizations that don't achieve their primary goal. If a church has a Sunday target attendance of 375 but the previous Sunday only 240 attended, the *Concern* is the gap between 240 and 375. If an insurance company normally processes 12,490 claims per week but last week processed 14,100, that's the *Concern*. Because these concerns are global—they affect the entire organization—the C4 worksheet is the best tool to use when working through them.

Step One: Understand the Current Situation

For someone to become proficient at the critical thinking C4 requires, he must first gain a general understanding of the big picture, including how his work contributes to the overall success of the company and its customers, and how things run within the firm. Tools like value stream mapping or process flow charts help show how things work together to accomplish the organization's goals. Understanding this true current state is vital, which is why it's so important to "go and see."

> *The controlled environment of a simulation is excellent for teaching most of the C4 process, but because, by definition, a simulation represents a discrete event of set duration, it is not a particularly data-rich environment. This limitation is important to note. In a real-world environment, data that have been properly collected and analyzed are essential for determining and prioritizing problems.*

As people populate their current state value stream maps, the right data is often missing because no meaningful targets or standards have been set. Thus, the first problem to solve: What data is needed? Once this problem is solved, examining the data collected is likely to reveal many other problems to be solved as well.

Data requirements flow from higher-level goals. The ultimate high-level goal, sometimes called the BHAG (for Big, Hairy Audacious Goal from Jim Collins's books, *Built to Last* and *Good to Great*), should accompany a vision statement that captures what the organization wants to become. A vision statement is different from the company's mission statement, which captures why the organization exists and what it does. In searching the web for compelling vision statements, we've found most organizations choose to focus on their mission rather than articulate a vision for the future. This spotlight may be deliberate, a preservation strategy designed to prevent awkward shifts due to factors often beyond that organization's control. For example, NASA had a great vision with a BHAG in 2009:

> At the core of NASA's future space exploration is a return to the moon, where [we] will build a sustainable long term human presence.

Since then, the changing political climate has killed funding for a sustainable lunar presence. NASA's vision had to change. Its big, overwhelming goal needed to come down to earth.

Rev-a-shelf, a producer of closet, cabinet and bathroom organizing inserts, has set its sights on operating within one building instead of the three it currently occupies. While this is the company's BHAG, the vision statement it's adopting is *"Innovation through Organization."* With this simple slogan Rev-a-shelf can communicate its priorities to everyone.

The company introduces around 150 new products a year, but it also emphasizes the importance of organizing the workplace for flow and visibility. Everyone in the company knows that his or her job is to improve the organization of the workplace or to be innovative in designing new products for the customer.

Starbucks is one of those companies that clearly states its mission—rather than its vision—on the company website. Even so, this mission is pretty lofty:

> *Our mission: to inspire and nurture the human spirit – one person, one cup and one neighborhood at a time.*

Articulating the company's vision and BHAG sets the stage for defining the key strategic objectives needed to realize that vision. These *strategic objectives* cascade to *objectives for value streams or departments* and then to *objectives for work centers*. The main idea is to drive the right behaviors in the workforce by explaining how the work each individual does contributes to the success of the company and monitoring ongoing performance so workers can take action whenever they see conditions go out of standard.

For now, the key question to ask in understanding the big picture is this: "Is this concern preventing us from realizing our vision?" If it's impossible to tell with the data available, start by defining some key metrics and collecting some data. As the problem becomes more clearly defined, it's important to note which current performance levels are relevant and then use the same set of metrics to note performance levels after *Countermeasures* are implemented. Comparing these before-and-after measurements is the only way to accurately determine if countermeasures have been effective.

The Concern section of the C4 worksheet—Understanding the current situation—offers a few guiding questions that flow from the main theme. They can be asked and answered in any sequence and will likely be asked several times as new answers are discovered and new evidence considered. As stated earlier, the key questions for any problem are:

Who? What? When? Where? How?

Answering these questions should lead to other questions that aren't written on the worksheet but still need to be asked and answered.

Concern: Understand the current situation	Use charts, diagrams, or photos whenever possible to describe the situation.	
Who discovered the problem? Gather findings from any previous studies of this problem area. Describe what is happening to indicate a problem. Describe the ideal condition. What standard is involved if any? When does this problem occur? How frequently? What is this problem costing the organization?	Current State Value Stream or Process Map. Summarize here, and indicate where others can find fully detailed map. What are the key problem areas on the map? (What are your angry clouds?)	Break down the larger problem. List the contributing problems below, sorting them by category. Attach an affinity diagram.

Who discovered the problem? Gather findings from any previous studies of the problem area.

It's important to know who discovered the problem, because this person is likely to have the most accurate knowledge about what was happening when the problem occurred. Sometimes the answer to "Who discovered the problem?" is obvious; at other times it isn't. If it's a global problem like the one discussed with the StrikeFighter (only 4 or 5 aircraft delivered against a requirement of 15) everyone tends to discover the problem together. When breaking down a big problem, it's important to ask the "who" question again and again, keeping in mind the importance of keeping the person who discovered the problem involved in the process.

It's not unusual to encounter some resistance when trying to find out who to talk to about problems. For hundreds of years most work environments have been places where it's been safer to hide problems, lest the person causing or discovering them be blamed and subsequently punished. Under the C4 system, problems are welcome; by solving them life improves for everyone. Making this clear, however, requires a fundamental shift in leadership.

Who?
- Who discovered the problem?
- Who is affected by the problem?
- Who can help identify and solve the problem?

What?
- What is happening to indicate a problem (what are the symptoms)?
- What standard is involved?

When?
- When does the problem occur? Frequency? Any particular patterns of occurrence? Timing?

Where?
- Where does the problem occur? Is it local or global?

How?
- How does the problem affect the organization?
- How costly is the problem to the organization?

Describe what is happening to indicate a problem. Surprisingly, coming up with this description stumps many people. The problem may be obvious, like delivering 4 or 5 units instead of 15, but group participants nearly always want to make this more complex than it really is. Here are a few examples of how a problem might be described on the C4 worksheet:

- I see smoke and smell a strong odor coming from the electric motor (manufacturing).
- I hear a knocking sound in the engine when I put the car in gear (driving).
- Nobody is buying the cherry cheesecake (restaurant).

- Patients are waiting over an hour before being called back to see the doctor (health care).
- I can't hit the bull's eye on the target (shooting).
- Customers aren't browsing very long (retail).
- We have too many reject parts (manufacturing).

The examples above are observations, based on what an individual has seen, heard, smelled, tasted or felt. They indicate a potential problem, though it's not yet obvious what the problem may be. This is the point in the process where it's important to define the current condition by capturing as many symptoms as possible. Later on, these symptoms can be critical in pinpointing or diagnosing the real problem.

Often data may be available that can further help

> **Concern: Understand the current**
>
> Who discovered the problem? Gather findings from any previous studies of this problem area.
> Prime contractor. No previous studies available.
>
> Describe what is happening to indicate a problem.
> Aircraft weren't ready when the customer came to pick them up. Everyone was waiting for materials.
>
> Describe the ideal condition. What standard is involved if any?
> We would deliver each aircraft, perfectly finished, just in time for delivery, with no excess materials
>
> When does this problem occur? How frequently?
> Aircraft are due 1 per minute beginning at minute 16. We could not build 1 per minute.
> What is this problem costing the organization?
>
> $137,400,000 on the 2.5 year contract.

to describe the problem. For example, if the company has been tracking equipment downtime, cherry cheesecake sales, patient waiting times or customer visit length, the data collected can help paint a picture of the current situation.

Generally, the simpler and more graphically information is recorded on the C4, the more impact that information is likely to have. The idea is not to make a chart just for sake of having one but to present data that is both useful and that can be interpreted quickly and easily.

Describe the ideal condition. What standard is involved if any? Describing the ideal condition provides a big-picture perspective, including whether or not there is a documented standard. If such a standard exists, it's important to say so. For example:

- Produce 40 good pieces per hour.
- Complete this section of the claim within 10 hours.
- See every patient within 10 minutes of arrival.
- Place three consecutive shots within a 3-cm circle in the center of the target.

When does this problem occur? How frequently? Identifying *when* the problem occurs is also important, because timing might reveal clues about the root *Cause*, which we'll examine in the next chapter. This question will also likely reveal instances when data collection is insufficient. Many of us experience problems at work, but usually we just work through them (or around them). If we never stop to document problems, we can't really tell if there is a pattern or frequency, such as if the problem only occurs on second shift, or only with a particular customer, or only during certain weather.

Complete a Current State Value Stream or Process Map. Summarize here and indicate where others can find the fully detailed map. In some cases, particularly those involving improvement projects, the next step in understanding the current situation is to create a value stream map, process flow map, or a spaghetti diagram to better see the whole process. (Be certain to record on the C4 worksheet where such maps can be found.)

There's no question that value stream mapping and analysis can be complicated, but many groups make it even more complicated than necessary. Use a facility map and trace the movements of people or products, as in the example to the right. (All the crossing lines are what give this spaghetti diagram its name.)

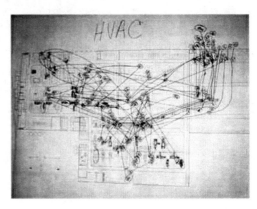

Spaghetti Diagram

For a simple value stream map, use a box to identify each process step, then lay out the boxes (called process boxes) left to right in the sequence required to complete the overall function. If two process steps are concurrent, arrange them one above the other. For each process box, gather key information about the particular step it represents (cycle time, changeover time, total work time available, number of operators, required materials). Use a triangle between the boxes to show the accumulation of work in process. This triangle can reflect partially assembled products or partially completed documents. *Go and see* to get an accurate count of the typical amount of in-process inventory.

The next step is to connect the process boxes with lines reflecting material and information flow. If one process step can work as hard and fast as possible, pushing products into a storage area where they will wait until needed for the next process step, draw a striped arrow to represent this "push" approach. If a process step has to wait until the next process step calls for additional product, use a looping arrow to represent this "pull" approach. Information flows are represented by thin, solid arrows. Connect the entire process to a customer and a supplier, then add a timeline along the bottom. On the example above, notice that the timeline is staggered. On the lower sections, record the time for value-added work.

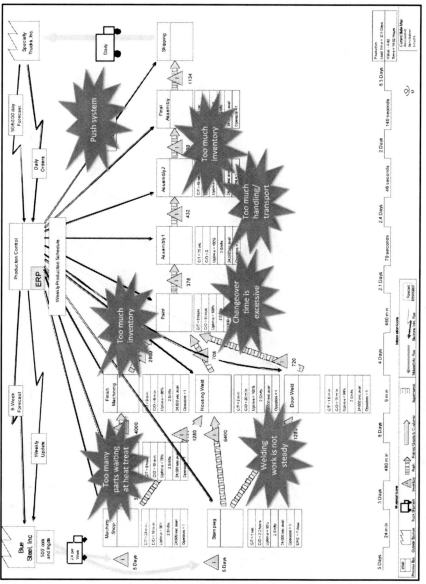

Current State Value Stream Map

In the case of concurrent processes, record the longest time. On the upper sections, record the time for non-value-added work. To the extreme right of the timeline, show a total non-value-added (NVA) time and a total value-added time, as well as the total processing time (the combination of NVA and value-added time).

Not every problem requires a value stream map, but to help break down larger problems it's a very useful tool. Once the map is complete, the next step is to identify some of the key contributing problems and add them to the map using a symbol like a starburst. The authors term these problems "angry clouds," because they're the things that usually make people angry.

What are the key problem areas on the map? (*What are the angry clouds?*) The diagram shown indicates several angry clouds. These issues will need to be addressed when developing a future state map in order to improve the overall work environment. The completed sample showing this portion of the C4 worksheet for StrikeFighter is shown above.

Break down the larger problem. List the contributing problems below, sorting them by category. Attach an affinity diagram.

The next step is to identify all contributing problems or barriers

---

nt situation   Use charts, diagrams, or photos wh

Current State Value Stream or Process Map. Summarize here, and indicate where others can find fully detailed map.

VSM pictures and details are in the file cabinet in the quality manager's office.

1A ▪A ▪B ▪A ▪B ▪B ▪C ▪D ▪D ▪C

2P▪ 3F▪   1C ▪ 3G▪ 2F   ▪ 3E ▪

What are the key problem areas on the map? (What are your angry clouds?)

Waiting for parts
Too much work in some work cells, not enough in others
Purchase orders took too long to complete
Truck drivers could not find parts

The Worm Pit

Most people would agree that wasting resources is a problem. When people are brainstorming to identify problems, a mnemonic device can often help them think through the entire environment in order to list as many concerns as possible. One of these mnemonic devices is known as the WORM PIT, an acronym created from the first letter of each of the seven types of waste usually found in the workplace.

W   – Waiting

O   – Overproduction

R   – Rework or rejects

M   – Motion

P   – Processing

I   – Inventory

T   – Transportation

Even though as a term worm pit is a fairly good memory jogger, people still have a hard time remembering a list. They're much more likely to remember a story, so here's the story of the worm pit:

Once upon a time, a company was busy working when they noticed they weren't making money. When they started to investigate, they discovered a large chunk of their company was missing. It had fallen into a deep, dark, dank and smelly pit filled with worms with big teeth and even bigger appetites. The worms were insatiable; they could eat as much as the company could pour into the pit. Unless the company stopped feeding the worms, the pit would grow deeper and wider until the entire firm collapsed into it, never to be seen again.

There's no way to completely avoid the worm pit, but it's vital to recognize the only way out of the pit is to stop wasting one of the most precious resources available to every organization: intellect. Harnessing the free creativity that all team members/associates bring to work with them every day is the best way to keep larger and larger pieces of the company out of the worm pit.

related to the larger problem, an activity that will generate more specific items to address. A structured brainstorming exercise like the 6-3-3 technique described in Chapter 1 is the most effective way to accomplish this task.

During these brainstorming exercises participants should be thinking about the sources of workplace problems—quality problems or other non-conformance issues, sources of variability in the process (temperature, pressure, humidity, time, moisture content, people, etc.), areas of higher cost, and safety issues. It's also important to consider the seven most common areas of waste—waiting, overproduction, rejects, motion, processing, inventory and transportation, as well as waste of the organization's most precious resource: intellect. See the story of the worm pit on the previous page for an easy way to remember these sources of waste.

At the conclusion of the brainstorming activity it's not unusual to be left with more than a hundred potential problems. For example, in the StrikeFighter activity, where the big problem or theme was delivery—4 aircraft delivered when 15 were due—participants generated the following 6-3-3 list (printed here in unedited form):

- Buildup of piece-part inventory throughout the process
- Main fuselage assembly very slow to final assembly
- Production flow was not consistent
- Suppliers aren't communicating
- Departments aren't very well organized
- No master schedule for suppliers
- Too much waiting
- Parts are in too many places
- Rework process was not known
- Couldn't tell if there was a part put on wrong

- Too much inventory
- Did not know the status of deliveries; how many we made, how many were left
- Did not track which aircraft number we were working on. Confusing when change orders hit
- Did not have the whole line working at the same pace
- Drivers did not know what they were supposed to be picking up
- Material load restrictions slowed the delivery of parts
- Some areas had more work to complete than others
- It was hard to find the parts we needed
- No cross-training between team members . . . could only work one station
- Warehouse was too far away
- Lots of clutter on the table. Couldn't tell which parts were samples and which were for production
- Our planning didn't include the other teams
- Parts were delivered in a pile that then had to be sorted by operators, causing delays
- No way to tell anyone when we got the wrong part delivered
- No communication to the suppliers
- Too much time spent picking parts
- No signal to produce the next item
- Need better time tracking of build/release
- Work cell balance untested
- Distance to customer too far
- Parts showing up in wrong quantities
- Parts bins were confusing
- Too many steps in the production process
- Delivery process to customer was assumed, not defined

- Did not track or log change orders well
- Did not problem-solve when parts ran out
- Team leader was working a critical part of the line. Couldn't help out anywhere else or solve any problems
- Quality guy was part of production (no one really inspecting his work, so he could be lying)
- Too many defects
- Overproduction of some components
- Purchase orders took too long to complete
- Customer didn't pick up the planes when they were done (planes due every minute, so customer picked up one per minute, instead of when they were ready)
- Couldn't maintain a steady pace
- Two drivers made pickup and delivery confusing. No one knew which driver was delivering which part
- Warehouses disorganized
- Excess capacity on the production line
- Engines produced ahead, not on demand
- Everyone delivered their subassemblies when they were done, not when the customer called for them. There were lots of subassemblies sitting in the prime contractor's warehouse at the end of the run
- Had to do a lot of rework on assemblies when we started going faster
- No one attending to supplier's warehouses. Everyone just had to pick through the inventory to get their parts
- Planes fell apart on delivery
- Final assembly couldn't keep up

Dozens of small concerns are contributing to the big *Concern*, though even the little ones seem to have had a big effect. Obviously, solving the big concern starts by solving the little ones. Since many of these small concerns are closely related, the most effective way to begin is to organize and prioritize them. The best tool for this activity is the affinity diagram.

> *A quick note on problems versus solutions:*
>
> *In brainstorming activities like the 6-3-3, people often describe what they wish had happened instead of stating the problem.*
>
> *Things like "no cross-training" or "no kitting in the warehouses" aren't problems; rather, they're implied solutions. Cross-training is a solution to a problem like "people could only work at one station without making defects." Kitting is a solution to "parts were delivered in a pile we had to sort through."*
>
> *Whenever you find yourself saying or writing, "We didn't have...," STOP. You're not really describing the problem; you're describing what you wish you had. Think through to the underlying problem. Write the problem. There will be time enough later to worry about solutions.*

The Toolbox

AFFINITY DIAGRAM

An affinity diagram is a tool used to organize a larger list of observations, potential problems, or potential solutions into a manageable set of problem groups. Such a list might be the product of the 6-3-3 exercise described earlier.

There are three key steps to completing an affinity diagram: *display, discuss* and *decide*.

1. *Display*: In this step, each team member writes his or her problem observations on sticky notes—one for each observation—then posts the notes on a board or on the wall. Next, team members arrange the notes (their own and others') into groups or clusters that sound related. For example, some of the concerns below relate to communicating with suppliers (1); others relate to parts (2).

    -   No communication with the suppliers (1)
    -   Too much time spent picking parts (2)
    -   No signal to produce the next item (1)
    -   Need better time-tracking of build/release (1)
    -   Work-cell balance untested
    -   Distance to customer too far
    -   Parts showing up in wrong quantities (2)
    -   Parts bins were confusing (2)

    It's important to avoid all discussion until each person has had a chance to categorize. Don't even eliminate duplicate notes unless they're precisely word for word, since sometimes people write observations that sound alike but actually refer to different problems. The idea is to foster an atmosphere free of *any* judgment so everyone feels free to write what's on his or her mind.

    After two or three people have posted their notes and arranged them into clusters, make a descriptive label for each cluster (maybe on a different colored sticky note). Sometimes it helps to use standard category labels like the 5 Ms (manpower, method, machines, materials and Mother Nature) or the 5 Ps (people, process, plant, parts and plan).

The more specific the label, the easier it is to articulate the problem to be solved. For example, a label like "Process" is very broad, whereas "Assembly Process Steps" clearly categorizes the area of concern. Or, instead of "Parts," it may be more effective to use "Picking Parts in Warehouses" or "Delivery of Parts to Work Centers."

Display: Step one of the affinity process

Sometimes team members come up with additional observations during the process of posting and categorizing the notes. If so, these observations should be noted and posted as well.

2. *Discuss*: During the second step of creating an affinity diagram, team members discuss each category, making sure the observations

posted belong in it. This discussion usually begins with an elimination of duplicates and/or frivolous notes and complaints and then turns to issues of significance. Which problem area was the biggest contributor to the project? Which one, if solved, would have the biggest impact on overall performance? To answer these questions it may be necessary to gather additional data through experimentation or question others to gain differing perspectives.

3. *Decide*: The purpose of all this discussion and data gathering is for the team to decide which concerns to work on first. Ideally the team will reach consensus on this point, which means *everyone agrees the decision was made with full consideration of all available input*. Consensus doesn't necessarily mean everyone agrees fully with the decision; it does mean all team members agree they can support the decision, even if they don't particularly like it. Consensus can be very difficult, especially for teams that haven't been together very long.

If a team is struggling to decide, multi-voting is a tool that often helps move the process along.

MULTI-VOTING

Among available decision-making tools, multi-voting is effective, fair, popular and easy. It's most useful when deciding among a long list of options, making it a perfect complement to the C4 process with its many problems in multiple clusters.

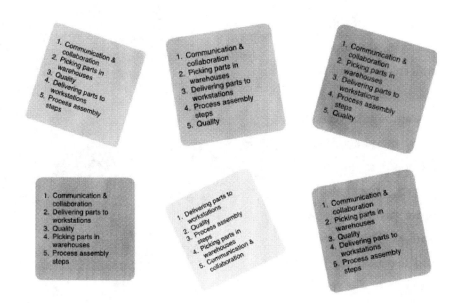

Category	Green	Orange	Blue	Purple	Gray	Yellow	Totals
Comm/Coll	1	1	1	1	1	5	10
Picking	2	4	2	2	2	4	16
Delivering	3	2	4	4	3	1	17
Process	4	5	5	5	4	3	26
Quality	5	3	3	3	5	2	21

Once the group has finished discussing the problems and sorted everything into labeled clusters, there are likely to be between five and seven clusters to choose from. Eventually, of course, *all* problems identified through the 6-3-3 exercise will need to be solved. The idea is to select the *most significant problem*, thus the one to be worked on first. Multi-voting is perfectly suited for this challenge.

There are two approaches to multi-voting. The first uses a rank-ordering technique. Based on experience, analysis or opinion, team members privately rank the five to seven clusters in order of importance, with #1 being the most important. One team member then collects the lists and publicly tallies the results. The cluster with the lowest total points becomes the top-priority item.

In the StrikeFighter example, the top-priority concern is related to *communication and collaboration* among the teams and team members. Next is picking parts in the warehouses, then delivering those parts to the workstations. Quality concerns and the assembly process round out the remaining categories.

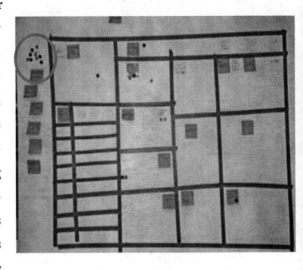

It's important to reiterate that *all* problems must be solved in order for aircraft to meet quality standards and be delivered on time. Multi-voting both provides a place to begin and helps to generate a priority list to use in meeting that goal.

The second multi-voting technique (both are equally effective, so which a team chooses is completely a matter of preference) gives each team member two, three or four votes to cast. Using different-colored markers or sticky dots, members cast votes however they wish. The problem category with the most votes becomes the top priority, followed by

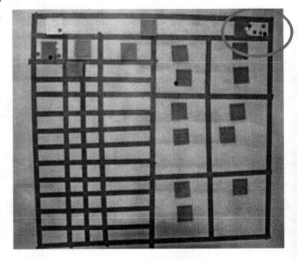

the second-highest vote getter and so on. It's important all team members vote at the same time to avoid having the person who goes last cast the deciding vote. Since avoiding this "deciding-vote factor" is often difficult, many groups prefer the rank-ordering system, even though the dot system is usually quicker.

The diagrams on the previous page show two different information-board layouts on which team members have placed dots to multi-vote for the features they prefer.

In these examples, after everyone selected his or her favorite features, the group worked together to create a new board incorporating them. The changes were then implemented in the shop.

Once a primary concern has been identified and agreed on, the next step is to create a problem statement.

The Problem Statement

As noted above, participants in the StrikeFighter example used the rank-ordering technique of multi-voting to identify *communication and collaboration* as their top-priority *Concern*. Their next task was to restate the problem in a simple, actionable problem statement before moving to the second stage in the C4 process, *Cause*. The most effective problem statements are both specific and data driven.

Problem statements can take one of four forms, depending on the nature of the problem:

- A statement of what the group wants to accomplish;
- A direct statement of effect;
- An aggressive goal; or
- A question that needs to be answered.

Here's an example of the four forms of a problem statement about the *communication and collaboration* concern of the StrikeFighter group:

- *Statement of what the team wants to accomplish:* We want all four teams to collaborate on the final solution and build a communication system that lets everyone know the status in real time.

- *Direct statement of effect:* Teams developed solutions without considering the needs of the enterprise.

- *Aggressive goal:* Within 90 minutes, develop an effective communication and transportation system that works for everyone.

- *Question:* How do we develop an effective communication and transportation system that works for everyone?

The statements above show multiple ways to phrase the same idea, but in real life it's only necessary to create one problem statement, written in whatever form resonates best with the team. Many groups like to include a statement of effect, which captures the current baseline, paired with an aggressive goal. This type of statement often encourages people to stretch, generating energy (motivation) for correcting the *Concern* and driving improvement through the company.

The box below contains a dozen problem statements generated by workers engaged in the C4 process in real-world work situations. The statements aren't perfect, but they don't need to be. Remember, the process is one of slop and magic—sometimes it's necessary to slog through the slop to find the magic. And every one of these "imperfect" problem statements contained enough magic for the teams that wrote them to accomplish their tasks.

This is a one of those times when the perfect can become the enemy of the good, so it's important not to get too wrapped up in generating the ideal problem statement. Teams that just keep slogging, rather than falling back on what they've always done, are teams that make progress.

The problem statements listed below were written by clients of the authors and have not been edited except for minor spelling corrections. Try to match each of them to one of the four problem-statement types:

> *a – statement of what the team wants to accomplish;*
> *b – statement of effect;*
> *c – aggressive goal; or*
> *d – question.*

1. Relocate accessories stock from mezzanine floor to the ground floor to eliminate travel time and OH & S issues.

2. To propose a standardized process that provides a clear indication of any discrepancies between what the customer ordered and what we are delivering in the most effective manner by 30 May 2010. As well as achieving a minimum 40% reduction in people and material movement, total process time and throughput time.

3. To create continuous flow of bulk stock from receiving into the high-rise. Other goals to achieve from doing this project will be to reduce interaction of forklifts and pedestrians and to eliminate frustration of looking for goods in the bulk area – happier workers. :-).

4. Implementation of a Standardized Daily Management Communication System within Technical Services to ensure efficient & effective communication across 2 shifts.

5. To improve the material handler's time for retrieving empties from 340 minutes to 160 minutes and to reduce the distance travelled in retrieving empties from 1,360 meters to 320 meters.

6. Improve the satisfaction measure of the Administration team by 22 without an increase in head count, and increase multi-skilling so that at least 90% of all tasks can be completed by at least two team members.

7. Reduce the setup time at Wrapping machine to 100 minutes from 300 minutes on an average.

8. Currently we achieve 76.7% of orders processed within 24 hours, by adopting this simple way of picking orders, I believe that we can achieve our goal of 95% of orders processed within 24 hours.

9. Our goal is to reduce material and people movement in the workstation by 30%, improve the work flow and reduce the amount of WIP from two days production worth to nearly a shift worth of stock.

10. Current printer paper supply is being pushed to inventory locations throughout corporate on a daily basis causing large on hand inventories and extra work for daily replenishment.

11. Reduce the number of damaged top and bottom sheets on veneer core loads by 50%.

12. Reduce Lockout/Tag out injuries by 50% by May 2011.

1 - a; 2 - c; 3 - a; 4 - a,d; 5 - b; 6 - c; 7 - c; 8 - b,c; 9 - c; 10 - b; 11 - c; 12 - c

After restating the *Concern*, redefine the current state, setting a performance baseline by collecting specific data about things like:

Walking distance	Defects, scrap, rework, errors
Inventory levels	Energy levels (electricity, gas, coal, etc.)
Lead time or cycle time	Paperwork
Work balance (time at each workstation in a work cell)	Output (products completed, reports filed, attendance levels, etc.)
Changeover/setup/startup time	Utilities (water, sewer)

Entering data into a table like the one shown below keeps things organized.

METRICS	Current State	Future State	Percent Improve-ment	METRICS	Current State	Future State	Percent Improvement
Safety: (near misses, trip hazards, etc.)				Cost: # of people in the process			
Quality: defects				People movements			
Delivery: # of material movements				People distance travelled			
Material travel distance				Square meters of floor space			
Material orientation losses							
Total processing time							
Total lead time							
Throughput time							

As explained further in Chapter 5, data also comes into play when developing *Countermeasures*. Effective countermeasures depend on early definition of evaluation factors, and problems supported by accurate data yield much better analysis.

C4 Worksheet Example: The StrikeFighter

Shown below is a completed *Concern* section of the C4 worksheet for the StrikeFighter simulation.

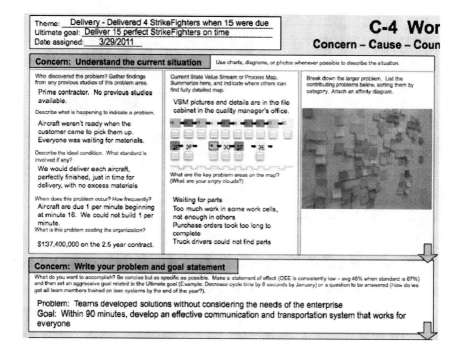

C4 Worksheet Example: Plywood Panels

Below is another completed *Concern* section, this time for the plywood mill discussed at the beginning of this chapter.

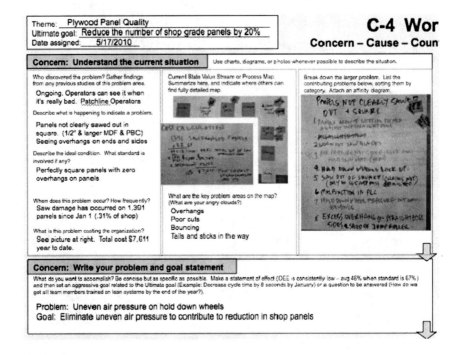

The plywood mill was experiencing too many panel defects. When panels come off the line they are inspected and designated as either on grade (they meet the high quality standards customers demand) or shop grade (they contain one or more serious defects). Shop-grade panels are sold at a deep discount and must be segregated from on-grade panels to prevent customer claims.

The team assigned to this problem worked in the mill where the panels were made, so they had control over the problem. The first step they took toward solving it was to participate in a brainstorming activity to break down the big problem or *theme* of "plywood panel quality" into smaller components. This activity exposed out-of-square panels as one of several different kinds of defects.

In answering the questions in the left-hand block of the C4 worksheet, the team needed specific data that wasn't readily available. To obtain this data it recorded the number of out-of-square panels produced per day for two types of composite wood panels (MDF and PBC). The data showed an average of 65 panels per week out of square, or a total of 3,381 panels over a 52-week period. Each of these panels must be sold at a $22 discount. The annual cost of this problem alone, one of dozens of types of defects, was $74,382.

The entire value stream map for processing plywood panels wouldn't help much in solving this problem, so the team decided to create a process map, which they documented with the photo shown on the next page. The following steps outline how a panel is created.

1. Veneer sheets are paired in tops and bottoms and collected in stacks of 24 pairs.

2. A core sheet (MDF and PBC in this case, but it could be any species of hardwood in a single panel or up to 5-ply panels) passes through a spreader that applies glue to both sides.

3. The core sheet lands on top of the bottom sheet.

4. A crew places the top sheet on top of the core sheet and repeats the process until a stack of 24 panels has been assembled.

5. The stack moves into the press, where it stays for several minutes to ensure the panels are bonded together.

The bonded panels then move to a pro-saw, which is where the process map begins. A feeder pushes each panel to the left edge of a conveyor, which aligns it as it goes into the saw (top photo). As panels pass through the pro-saw, both sides of the panel are sawed out simultaneously. To hold panels steady during this process, they're held down by roller wheels (bottom photo).

After passing through the pro-saw, the panels are immediately rolled (one at a time) to another conveyor where a second blade set saws off the ends using the same feeding, holding and sawing process.

Panels are then restacked and moved to the patch line, where they are inspected and defects on each side corrected by patching with putty and resanding. The patched panels are then graded and stacked by an automatic stacker/sorter into lots of on-grade and shop-grade product, which are strapped, labeled and shipped.

The key problems identified by the team were overhangs (shown at right), poor cuts, bouncing panels, and tails and sticks (pieces that had been cut off the panel) getting in the way.

Breaking down the problem of out-of-square-panels, the team listed the following:

- Panels not pushed against the straightedge
- Worn-out saw blades
- Uneven air pressure on hold-down wheels
- Hold-down wheels lock up
- Saw out of square on second pass saw (chains not aligned)
- Malfunction in the PLC
- Hold-down-wheel pressure out of sequence
- Excess overhang on straight-edge sides
- Speed of the jump roller

These problems are all related to the problem of out-of-square panels. One or more of them could be *Causes*, but at this point the task is to identify the *Concern*, the primary problem to solve. As the team investigated each of these problems, searching for actual occurrences, it discovered there was little data available. Using the "go and see" recommendation discussed earlier, the team went to the saw and spent several hours observing the process and making notes.

After discussing their observations, they decided to use multi-voting to select the priority problem. "Uneven air pressure on hold-down wheels" received the most votes, so they recorded this as the problem statement and moved to the next stage of the C4 process: *Cause.*

CHAPTER 4

Cause: Thinking to the Source

The previous chapter dealt with the first stage of the C4 process, *Concern*. The *Concern* step provides a method for sorting through multiple symptoms to identify the actual problem, breaking down the problem into many smaller problems, and identifying which of these problem components is the main problem or top priority. This chapter explores how to find the *Cause* of that problem. Chapter 5 discusses *Countermeasures*—ways to solve problems—but applying a countermeasure to a problem without knowing the underlying, fundamental causes is almost certain to fail, if not immediately then over time. Effective problem solving aims to eliminate the problem permanently by focusing squarely on the root cause.

Several tools exist to help identify the root cause of a problem. Three that are particularly useful include:

- The 5 whys
- Fishbone cause-and-effect diagrams
- Stem-and-leaf cause analysis

Although these tools have been proven effective, are well publicized and have been used for years, many organizations avoid them in an effort to put in place quick solutions to sometimes painful problems. In contrast, the C4 process relies on them heavily. In fact, C4 participants must do a step-by-step completion of the 5 whys and at least one of the other two, forcing them to take their time and do the analysis up front instead of jumping into the trial-and-error pursuit of a short-term solution. Each of these three tools is discussed below.

Note that it's usually fairly easy to begin with the 5 whys, but *the authors do not recommend it for larger problems,* because it can be very difficult to reach an actual root cause with this method. Just as the *Concern* stage of C4 helps break down a large problem by asking, "What are all the problems associated with . . .," the fishbone or stem-and-leaf techniques will generate a small number of potential root causes. In fact, many of the smaller problems that came up during the *Concern* stage will show up again here. The main difference is that this step asks, "What *caused* the problem we're trying to solve?"

Both the fishbone and stem-and-leaf techniques require continuously asking "Why?" as the group works through all potential causes and identifies one, two or three as priorities. The 5 whys can then be applied just to these priority causes.

> *Few problems have just one root cause; in fact, most have multiple, interacting causes that must be addressed. It's important, therefore, not to get hung up on finding a single root cause.*

In the StrikeFighter example, the large problem was delivering only 4 out of the required 15 aircraft. Asking what problems were associated with this problem brought forth dozens of contributing problems, including the much more focused problem that *teams developed solutions without considering the needs of the enterprise.* Because teams developed solutions without considering the needs of the enterprise, the integrated system failed; therefore, the group was unable to deliver the 15 aircraft required. Clearly the process of identifying causes begins in the *Concern* stage. The *Cause* stage provides additional tools, tools that help isolate specific root causes for which *Countermeasures* can be developed and applied.

The Toolbox

5 Whys

Five whys gets its name from old books about Toyota and the Toyota Production System,[1] where key individuals like Taiichi Ohno and Shigeo Shingo taught that to get to the root cause of most problems in a factory, it's important to ask why they happened and to *keep asking why at least five times.*

Most people agree 5 whys is a fairly simple concept, but in today's workplace it's often misapplied, misunderstood, or simply missed altogether. Here are some examples of how this tool is often misapplied.

- Asking 5 whos instead of 5 whys. Instead of looking for the cause, the questioner is looking for someone to blame.
- Asking why 5 times, but asking more or less the same question, thus generating five different, unrelated responses. For example: *We missed our production target today.*

  1. *Why?* Because machine 34 was down for two hours.
  2. *Why?* Because we had one man absent and two out on an improvement team.
  3. *Why?* Because we ran out of materials.

---

1 Taiichi Ohno, *Workplace Management.* Productivity Press: New York (1988). Hardcover copies are very expensive and somewhat rare, but a paperback version was released a couple of years ago.

4. *Why?* Because we had to spend 45 minutes extra after the team meeting updating our information board.

5. *Why?* Because it took another 20 minutes to fill out the C4 card the superintendent asked for.

- Asking why but guessing or estimating the answers instead of using a "go and see" strategy to find the truth.
- Asking why a fourth or fifth time, when the cause was exposed after the second.

> *The number five in the 5 whys is just a guide. It's important to keep asking until you get to the root cause, whether it takes 2 whys or 20 whys. How do you know you're finished? Keep reading.*

To make 5 whys work takes discipline, data and determination. Asking why is the easy part. Answering is the hard part.

When a problem occurs it's only human nature to want to find someone to blame, but finding this person rarely addresses the real concern. Punishing people for causing a problem makes it less likely they'll be forthcoming about the next problem they discover; and the original problem remains unsolved.

If everyone in an organization is not earnestly looking for problems in workplace systems, the company will *never* achieve the performance levels of which it's capable. Working in an environment where people are afraid to try something new for fear of failing puts too much of a burden on managers who usually have little real expertise in the hands-on work for which they are ultimately responsible. Fear-driven organizations are not innovative. They don't solve problems as a routine daily activity and they don't develop people's skills properly to make the organization nimble. In other words, fear prevents companies from becoming learning organizations. If a company can't solve problems it can't innovate. If it can't innovate it will cease to be competitive, especially in today's integrated global economy.

To execute 5 whys properly, it's important both to state the questions clearly and to gather data to support the answers. For example: *We missed our production target today.*

1. *Why did we miss our production target?*

    A: Machine 34 was down for two hours.

2. *Why was machine 34 down for two hours?* (Factual answers to this question should be available.)

    A: Because it had an oil leak at the main hydraulic connector that took two hours to fix. This answer points to two areas of inquiry: the oil leak, which will lead to one cause, or the two-hour repair time, which is a different problem with a different cause. For simplicity, the following "whys" concentrate on the oil leak.

3. *Why did machine 34 have an oil leak at the main hydraulic connector?*

    A: Because the seal showed signs of abnormal wear: It looked like the hose near the connector had been hit with a parts cart.

4. *Why did a parts cart hit the hose?*

    A: Because the hose is very close to the water spider's replenishment route, and the cart can sometimes roll into the machine. (Some companies refer to the internal parts replenishment person as the "water spider" because he or she is constantly in motion, moving from station to station.)

5. *Why does the cart sometimes roll into the machine?*

   A: Because the machine is close to the water spider's route.

The answer to the fifth "why?" has started a loop-back to the previous answer. Other answers might have been "because the water spider doesn't always pay attention" or "because the water spider goes faster when he gets behind and sometimes loses control." Some groups continued down this path, ultimately ending with something like "because management never told us to." This conclusion might satisfy the urge to blame someone, especially when exposing another management shortcoming, but it's not an actionable cause, particularly considering the original problem is machine downtime. Since any action taken ultimately needs to reduce downtime, the answer to the fourth why?—the cart can sometimes roll into the machine—should be recorded as the root cause.

One technique that helps groups ensure their answers make sense is to work the 5 whys backward to the original problem, using declarative statements and the transitional term *therefore* to check the logic of the path. Here's an illustration of this principle as applied to the example above.

- The cart can sometimes roll into the machine; and   *therefore*
- The parts cart hit the hydraulic hose; and   *therefore*
- There is an oil leak at the main hydraulic connector; and   *therefore*
- Machine 34 was down for two hours; and   *therefore*
- We missed our production target.

This approach isn't very scientific, but it forces the group to think through the logical connections it's trying to establish. If an answer doesn't make sense, it's probably wrong.

How does a group know when it's reached the root cause and thus is finished with the 5 whys? Here are a few indications.

1. When the only remaining answer blames someone other than the team, e.g., "because management hasn't given us the time to do standardized work";

2. When the only answer loops back to an earlier answer, as in the machine downtime example above; and/or

3. When the only answer leads to something on which the team itself cannot take action, e.g., "because the machine is designed that way."

This methodology of asking why repeatedly is also used with the tools described next, the fishbone cause-and-effect diagram and the stem-and-leaf cause analysis.

Fishbone Cause-and-Effect Diagram

The fishbone diagram, so called because its basic structure resembles the simplified skeleton of a fish, has been used by problem solvers since the 1940s, though it wasn't until the total quality movement (TQM) that it reached the masses, thanks to Kaoru Ishikawa, a professor in Japan, who described it in several books and papers in the late 1980s. Consequently, some quality manuals refer to the fishbone diagram as the Ishikawa diagram.

This tool works best in a group setting. To use it, write the problem statement on the diagram and ask "What caused this?" or "Why did this happen?" In most cases, the *Concern* statement is a statement of effect, for example, "Machine 34 had two hours of downtime yesterday." Sometimes the problem statement is a goal or question, for example: "We need to reduce overall downtime by 15 percent," or "How do we get all team members trained on reducing downtime?" In this case it might be necessary to change the question in the *Cause* stage from "What caused this?" to "What are the barriers to achieving this?"

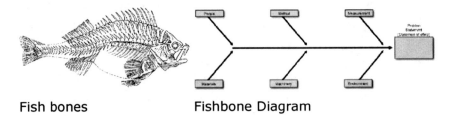

Fish bones   Fishbone Diagram

As indicated in the diagram above, the *Concern*, goal or target is written clearly at the head of the diagram on the right (the diagram, of course, is ambidextrous and could point in the opposite direction, depending on the user's preference). It's helpful for groups to label the ends of each of the "bones," if only to allow the brain to focus more specifically on one area of the cause at a time. Favorites for labels include the 5 Ms (manpower, method, machines, materials and Mother Nature) or the 5 Ps (people, process, plant, parts and plan), but there is no need to limit discussion to these areas. Whatever set of labels a group selects to begin with can be adjusted as the discussion progresses. Other labels might include: environment, measurement, money, performance, logistics, paperwork, time, vehicles or anything else relevant to the particular problem. The C4 worksheet has a standard set labeled people, method, measurement, environment, machinery and materials.

Once the *Concern* or problem statement is recorded at the "head" of the fish and the "bones" are labeled, the group can begin to populate the diagram. There are different ways to accomplish this task. One group may decide simply to hold an unstructured brainstorming session, recording suggested causes where they seem to fit. A more structured approach, however, is likely to generate better results.

Completing this diagram first requires focusing the group on the concern and then on the specific fishbone label (e.g., *people*). As participants make suggestions in response to a question like "What people issues may have caused this problem?" it's possible to create a logic path by repeatedly asking "What caused this?" and using the answers to build branches off the main fishbone. The basic premise is the same as that of the 5-why analysis: Keep asking why something happened.

The example below shows the branches generated with this structured approach. Follow the logic path under the fishbone labeled *method*:

Excessive departure delays (the *Concern*)

> caused by interior servicing delays

>> caused by late service crew

>>> caused by too many aircraft to service

>>>> caused by recent staff reductions.

Working through the fishbone in this way may expose a priority cause, especially if the same cause—something like "Recent staff reductions to save cost"—shows up at the end of multiple logic paths.

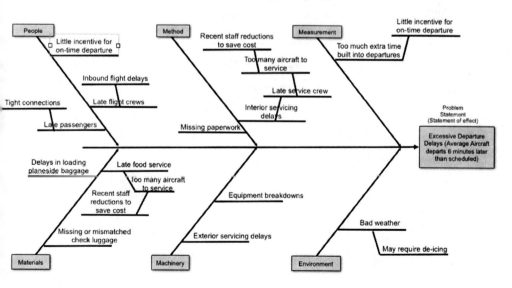

Excessive departure delays represent a very large concern and would benefit from being broken down in the same way as the StrikeFighter delivery concern. Without this interim step, it's extremely difficult to identify what might have caused the problem, and the fishbone diagram can get quite complex.

The hardest part of the process at this point is confirming that suggested causes are true. This verification requires additional data collection and analysis and is very likely to require structured experimentation to replicate the problem. In short, groups cannot assume causes. They must confirm them.

Once the group has identified two or three priority causes, C4 recommends taking each through its own 5-why analysis. If the group did a good job on the fishbone, it may get to only one or two whys before finishing, but completing this step provides a simple sanity check for the work done so far.

The fishbone diagram on the following page shows another example of this method in action. In this case, the technique was used to capture causes of downtime on a particular robot.

Some groups find the fishbone challenging, specifically stating that it's often very difficult to isolate a root cause. The success of this technique is a function of the effectiveness of brainstorming activity, data collection, and the construction of logic paths. With accurate data and rigorous analysis, the fishbone can be extremely successful. Nonetheless, some groups prefer the stem-and-leaf approach.

STEM-AND-LEAF CAUSE ANALYSIS

The logic or critical thinking requirements for the stem-and-leaf are the same as for 5 whys or the fishbone. The idea is to identify and examine

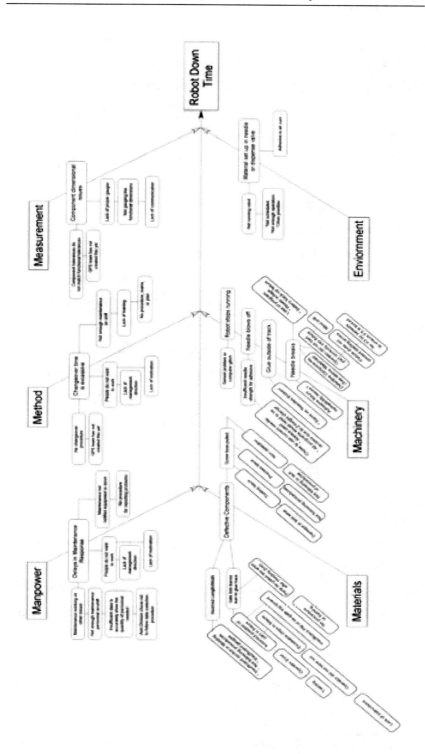

potential causes in a deliberate manner, continuing to ask "Why did this happen?" until reaching the root causes. The difference between stem-and-leaf analysis and the other methods discussed is that this technique focuses on eliminating suggested causes early in the process.

The exercise begins by recording the problem at the start or "stem" of a diagram. Branching out from that stem, the group records different potential causes or "leaves" on separate lines or in separate boxes. Each leaf should connect logically: *The stem is caused by the leaf.* In the book *Apollo Root Cause Analysis*,[2] the author suggests writing "caused by" on each of the connecting lines to make these relationships clear. He also recommends recording the source of evidence of the cause below each "leaf."

The group continues to build a logic path by identifying additional potential causes specific to each leaf. (Again, boxes for these causes should be connected to the previous box with a "caused by" line.) As each potential cause is reviewed, the group seeks to identify information to prove or disprove it as a cause of the problem, eliminating disproved causes from further consideration. Gathering information to make these calls might require controlled experimentation and data analysis, which is one of the reasons this technique is so powerful. Eventually the group reaches a point where the data collected and analyzed confirms that a specific leaf contributed to the problem. This leaf then becomes the priority root *Cause*.

In this sample diagram, the group identified three potential causes of the selected problem but was able to eliminate Potential Cause 1 right away. Asking what caused Potential Cause 2 generated three more potential causes; exploring Potential Cause 3 identified two more potential causes. By analyzing these five new potential causes, the group was able to eliminate a, b and f, leaving two potential root *Causes*. Asking what caused these, the group identified two more potential causes for Potential Cause c, and one more for Potential Cause e. After still more data collection and

2   Dean L. Gano, *Apollo Root Cause Analysis: A New Way of Thinking*. Apollonian Publications: Yakima, WA (1999).

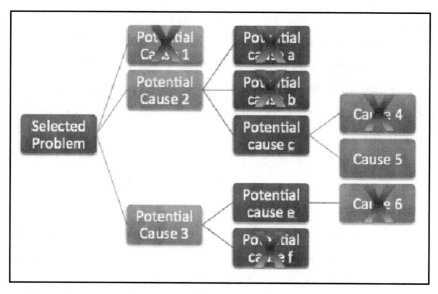

analysis, Causes 4 and 6 were eliminated, leaving Cause 5 as the root cause of the problem. An actual example is shown below.

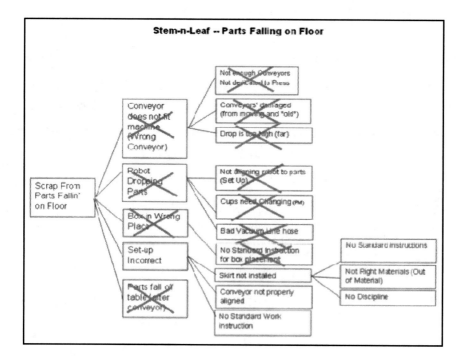

In the case represented by this diagram, shown here exactly as produced by the group that worked on it, parts coming out of a mold are falling on the floor and have to be scrapped. The group documented a loss of over $26,000 per month due to scrapped parts. The first round of questioning identified five potential causes and eliminated one—parts fall off table (after conveyor).

Through further exploration, the group identified ten additional causes for the remaining four initial causes. It was then able to eliminate seven of them, ending up with three priority *Causes*:

1. Skirt not installed, which was further broken down into three more causes.
2. Conveyor not properly aligned.
3. No standard work instruction (for setup).

Next the group ran a 5-why analysis on its three priority causes. The conclusions were as follows: If the skirt beneath the mold was properly installed and the conveyor properly aligned, both of which should be included in the standardized work for setup of the mold, scrap caused as a result of parts hitting the floor would be reduced to nearly zero.

The root causes in these examples are relatively straightforward. Determining true root causes for problems like the Deep Water Horizon disaster in the Gulf of Mexico in 2010 or the failure of multiple, redundant backup power supplies at the Fukushima nuclear plant in the wake of the Japanese earthquake and tsunami in 2011 may take years. Some causes may never be found; there simply isn't enough evidence to run the logic path to its true end.

The results of either a fishbone diagram or a stem-and-leaf diagram should be transferred to the Cause: Analysis block on the C4 worksheet. The group may either take a picture of the larger charts used and paste them to the worksheet, or reproduce the diagram by hand.

Cause: Analysis	Brainstorm and organize potential causes or obstacles using the Fishbone diagram, stem-and-leaf diagram, or other organizing tool. Write the causes of the problem or obstacles to improvement in the space provided, always verifying that what you record is an actual CAUSE of the problem.				
Priority Causes	What else?	Who else?	When?	Evaluation	Rank order

At the bottom of this block is the priority causes table. Opposite each priority (root) cause are several columns:

- **What else?** What, if any, additional information is needed to confirm this as a priority cause?
- **Who else?** In addition to members of the group, who may need to get involved in the process to ensure the analysis was accurate and effective?
- **When?** When does this supplemental information need to be available to the group?
- **Evaluation?** How does the group intend to evaluate the information to determine which of the causes listed is the top priority.
- **Rank order?** If necessary, once the additional analysis is complete, the group can rank the priority causes in order from most to least important.

Just because there are only two lines on the worksheet doesn't mean further review is limited to two causes. If analysis shows three or four mutually exclusive factors that are causing the selected problem, the group should analyze each to decide which to attack first. However, once a group has thoughtfully and accurately completed either the fishbone or stem-and-leaf, the resulting causes should be clear and the priority largely evident.

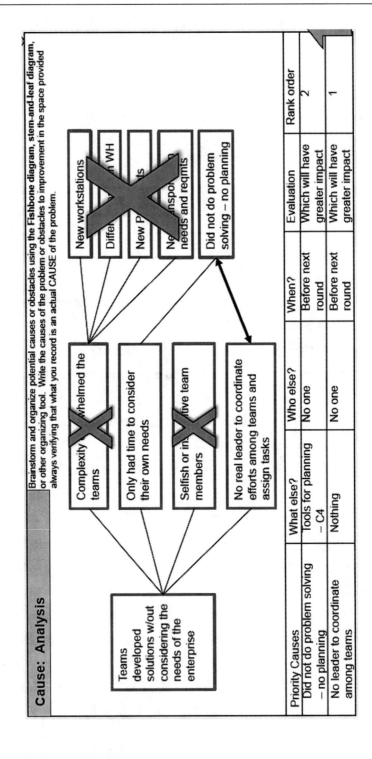

Cause: Analysis

Brainstorm and organize potential causes or obstacles using the **Fishbone diagram, stem-and-leaf diagram,** or other organizing tool. Write the causes of the problem or obstacles to improvement in the space provided always verifying that what you record is an actual CAUSE of the problem.

New workstations

Differ__ __ WH

New P__ __ts

Ne__ nspo__
needs and reqmts

Did not do problem
solving – no planning

Complexity __whelmed the
teams

Only had time to consider
their own needs

Selfish or in__tive team
members

No real leader to coordinate
efforts among teams and
assign tasks

Teams
developed
solutions w/out
considering the
needs of the
enterprise

Priority Causes	What else?	Who else?	When?	Evaluation	Rank order
Did not do problem solving – no planning	Tools for planning – C4	No one	Before next round	Which will have greater impact	2
No leader to coordinate among teams	Nothing	No one	Before next round	Which will have greater impact	1

C4 Worksheet Example: The StrikeFighter

The problem recorded in the left-most block of the StrikeFighter example on the previous page flows word for word from the Concern block of the worksheet. Here the group identified four potential causes, then eliminated "selfish or insensitive team members" because it believed everyone had good intentions.

When exploring the causes of complexity, the group cited the new requirements included in the second round of the simulation. However, since new requirements are inevitable in any organization—sometimes a result of customer demand, other times due to organizational change—it decided to eliminate complexity as a root cause, focusing instead on "only had time to consider their own needs" and "no real leader to coordinate efforts among teams and assign tasks." When team members asked what caused these problems, the only truthful answer was that they didn't use their time wisely. Instead of problem solving, they jumped directly into solution mode, trying one thing and then another. When they asked what caused this, the best answer appeared to be because they didn't have a leader who stopped them, got them focused on working together, assigned tasks and held people accountable. This is why the diagram shows a two-headed arrow on the caused-by line connecting the "no real leader" and "no problem solving/planning" boxes.

Both "did not do problem solving – no planning" and "no leader to coordinate among teams" are listed as priority causes. The team thought it could improve its planning and problem-solving skills by simply examining the tools more closely and getting other team members involved. On the other hand, members believed a leader would provide more direction and structure. Therefore, this was selected as the number one priority.

Here's the Cause: 5 Why Analysis block for the StrikeFighter

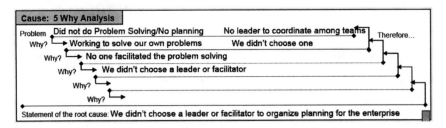

C4 Worksheet Example: Plywood Panels

In the *Concern* stage, the team working on this problem identified "uneven air pressure on hold-down wheels" as the specific problem to solve. Further analysis yielded two key causes: "operator error" and "pressure drops (equipment failure)." Unable to eliminate either without clearer definition, the group dug deeper.

Half the team addressed pressure drops; half addressed operator error.

Exploring why pressure would drop to the hold-down wheels, the team looked at three potential causes.

1. Does increased plant-wide demand at certain times of the day contribute to the problem?
2. Could air leaks in the system contribute to the problem?
3. Have compressor failures contributed to the problem?

While conducting their investigation, members learned that maintenance records for the compressor that serviced this part of the mill showed no abnormal failures and no failures at all during the time period on which the team was focused. Compressor failures, therefore, could be eliminated as a potential cause.

Next, the team went through the mill in search of air leaks. None were found—another potential cause eliminated. Finally, after checking plant-wide demand for air pressure, the team determined high

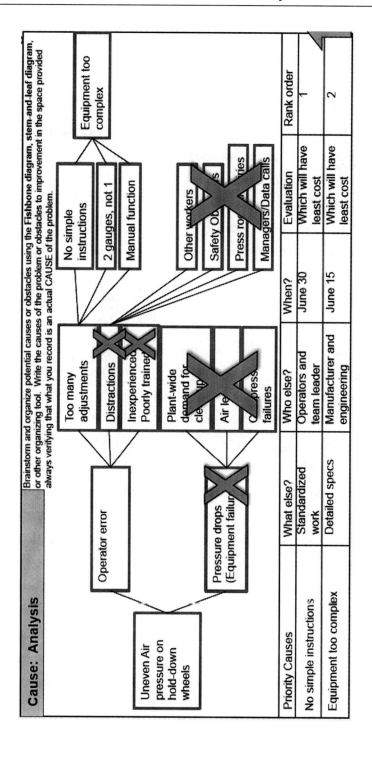

Cause: Analysis

Brainstorm and organize potential causes or obstacles using the **Fishbone diagram, stem-and-leaf diagram,** or other organizing tool. Write the causes of the problem or obstacles to improvement in the space provided always verifying that what you record is an actual CAUSE of the problem.

Equipment too complex

No simple instructions
2 gauges, not 1
Manual function

Other workers
Safety Ob~~~~s
Press ro~~~~ries
Managers/Data calls

Too many adjustments
Distractions
Inexperienced
Poorly trained

Plant-wide demand for cle~~~p
Air le~~
C~~ press failures

Operator error

Pressure drops (Equipment failur~~)

Uneven Air pressure on hold-down wheels

Priority Causes	What else?	Who else?	When?	Evaluation	Rank order
No simple instructions	Standardized work	Operators and team leader	June 30	Which will have least cost	1
Equipment too complex	Detailed specs	Manufacturer and engineering	June 15	Which will have least cost	2

demand was an issue only at the end of the day after the entire plant had completed its assigned production work and was using compressed air to clean equipment. Since the saw did not run at this time, this potential cause was eliminated as well.

Team members addressing operator error identified three primary contributors: too many adjustments to make for the hold-down wheels, too many distractions preventing the operator from focusing on the setup, and inexperienced operators.

A review of training records for the operators revealed each had more than 12 years of service and every operator had met all training requirements. Thus poor training and/or inexperience was not the cause of the problem. The group was also concerned about several sources of distraction: other workers, safety observations, press room queries (the saw is immediately downstream of the press room) and managers looking for information. Considering human nature and company requirements, the group decided there was very little it could do to eliminate these distractions. While it might make sense to issue a statement encouraging everyone to minimize distractions, the distractions themselves were not a valid root cause. This left "too many adjustments."

When asked why there were too many adjustments, operators replied there were no simple instructions to follow, there were two gauges to check (on opposite sides of the machine), and setup was manual, requiring adjustment by hand. When the group asked why these things were so, the only answers pointed to the design of the machine and the fact that operators hadn't developed any instructions to follow. The team concluded the problem of "uneven pressure on hold-down wheels" resulted from the priority *Causes* of "no simple instructions" and "equipment too complex," and that it was within their control to develop *Countermeasures* for the problem.

The next step was to run a 5-why analysis on each of the priority causes. The results for "no simple instructions" are shown below.

No simple instructions

> Because the standardized work has too many steps and small writing

> Because we're trying to capture too many functions on one set of instructions

> Because the equipment requires many adjustments in many places

Since the analysis of this option looped into the other priority cause, equipment complexity, the team stopped there. The answer to "Why does the equipment require many adjustments in many places?" is "because that's the way the equipment is designed," which is not an actionable answer. The team could provide feedback to the equipment manufacturer, but in the meantime local, immediate action was needed to reduce the number of out-of-square panels, the original problem the team had been charged with solving.

The root cause of this problem, then, is that the equipment requires too many adjustments in too many places for operators to consistently ensure perfect quality.

The Cause: 5 Why Analysis block for the plywood panels example looks like this:

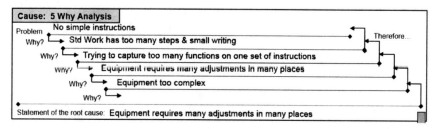

Once the root *Cause(s)* for a problem have been determined, it's time to develop *Countermeasures*, which are discussed at length in the following chapter.

CHAPTER 5

Countermeasure: Developing Permanent Solutions

Chapter 3 discussed how to identify the *Concern*—in other words, the "real" problem. Chapter 4 reviewed tools for determining the root *Cause* of that problem. Now it's time to solve the problem by applying one or more effective *Countermeasures*. Simply defined, a countermeasure is an action that corrects a problem at its root cause. The C4 system for developing effective countermeasures consists of the following five steps:

- Contain
- Formulate
- Evaluate
- Plan
- Implement

Contain

From the days of the total quality movement (TQM), quality processes such as FMEA (failure mode and effects analysis) and ISO 9001 have emphasized the need for containment and corrective action in addressing the problem of defects. This language is deeply ingrained in many organizations, but for the C4 process, we're shifting to a single term: *Countermeasure*. This small shift in terminology represents a big shift in thinking for sustainable improvements.

Under C4, taking action to *contain* a problem is just a short-term countermeasure. It's meant to be an immediate, reactive response, but it doesn't necessarily address the problem itself. It's like putting an adhesive bandage on a cut. Hopefully, the bandage keeps the cut from getting worse, but it's no help at all in finding out what caused the cut or how to prevent it from happening again. The long-term countermeasure replaces *corrective action*. It's meant to be a permanent solution. Countermeasures capture the reality that all attempts to deal with a problem may not be corrective. Some actions may be preventive or inventive, as well.

When a problem is discovered, it's important to take immediate action to *contain* it so it doesn't affect other products and/or other parts of the organization. Sometimes this means stopping production or delivery long enough to ensure the processes affected aren't going to create even more problems. Problems that have an impact on productivity, whether in a factory, office or hospital, are often particularly costly.

One of the examples cited in Chapter 4 concerned the problem of parts needing to be scrapped because they hit the floor coming out of a mold. In this case, a short-term countermeasure might involve placing a box under the mold to catch the parts, or making sure the box was positioned properly beneath the mold, or replacing a full box with an empty box. In each instance—unless there is another safety issue that would prevent positioning the box under the mold in the first place—such adjustments could be made during the regular production cycle. As illustrated in the previous chapter, however, the number of potential causes for this problem is significant. Simply continuing to adjust the box, or making sure an operator checks the box position every 10 minutes, is like putting the adhesive bandage on the cut. Neither solution addresses the real problem, nor does it deal with the real causes. In other words, nothing has happened to make the problem stop happening.

Stopping production is a traumatic experience, which is probably why people seem very good at applying short-term countermeasures to get things working again. What most people are not as committed to is following up, digging into the causes of the problem, and developing effective long-term countermeasures. Part of this reluctance could be a function of the increasing levels of "busy-ness" most people experience at work. Many companies are operating with the exact number of people needed when things are working correctly. When something goes wrong, by definition employees are already overextended. It's not surprising that many people—workers and managers alike—argue they have neither the time nor the manpower to conduct a more thorough problem analysis. The adhesive bandage approach will have to do.

In lean companies, follow-up is the job of the team leader. Typically this individual is not assigned to a workstation and thus is free to respond to problems as they occur or to help other workers as needed.

Making the pitch for installing a team-based work structure with team leaders is a topic for another time but, regardless of internal structure, if companies don't run problems to their root *Causes* and develop permanent countermeasures, they'll keep losing time to the same concerns, over and over again. Taking time to solve the problem when it's discovered saves countless hours down the road.

A small caution. In the parts-on-the-floor example described above, no one is recommending workers stop the machine immediately when they see a part hit the floor. It makes much more sense to apply a short-term countermeasure until the end of the scheduled production run, provided the run is relatively short and there is low probability of losing more parts to the scrap bin. Amplifying disruption in the work area doesn't solve problems; it simply creates more of them. It's much more logical to use critical thinking (who, what, when, where, how) to decide when to shut down and when to wait until the next normal break.

> *A large manufacturing company went to great lengths to conduct lean training for the entire production workforce. Trainers emphasized the need to "stop the line" if anyone discovered a problem. The operators thought this was a great idea. Back at work after the training, the first time they discovered a problem (which they did almost immediately) they stopped production, notified the line manager by activating their new andon system, and took a break "until the problem is fixed." Obviously the training failed to emphasize a critical component of lean: the problem belongs to the discoverer! After reporting the problem, the person who found it must immediately begin working on a solution. Everyone in the organization, not just managers, needs to develop these problem-solving and critical-thinking skills.*

If a short-term countermeasure fails to correct the situation, even for a short time, the only option is to stop and fix the true problem.

It important to record any short-term countermeasures applied. This historical record of problems and actions taken will help with future diagnoses and solutions should the countermeasure fail or a related problem occur. C4 cards and worksheets provide relatively easy forms on which to document problems and countermeasures. Restructuring operations to put in place one-piece flow with self and successor checks (quality at the source), and andon systems to notify everyone when a problem occurs, will drive down the number and severity of defects in any process. It will also reduce the need for containment inspections and segregation of large batches of potentially defective products. However, implementing these changes requires a corresponding change in leadership and behavior expectations. Changing one side of the equation without changing the other means neither will work for very long.

Formulate

EVALUATION CRITERIA

The first step in formulating countermeasures is to decide how to evaluate them. In an ideal world, a team will generate several different and creative countermeasures to the problem and then decide which are most viable by evaluating them against a set of defined criteria. In the real world, this approach presents several challenges.

1. Human beings like to get straight to the solution. We thrive on the action associated with trial and error, often overlooking its accompanying frustration, which we're happy to leave in the hands of an expert. If the expert is lucky enough to find a solution quickly, everyone celebrates.

2. Teams tend to create a list of things they could implement as countermeasures but quickly discover they need to implement *everything* on the list for the countermeasure to be effective. In other words, there really weren't multiple approaches to evaluate, just the same kind of thinking that caused the problem in the first place.

There is no magic about selecting evaluation criteria. Back in the *Concern* stage, groups define the concern and gather a set of data to serve as a measurement baseline. Many of these same data points often serve as evaluation criteria or as building blocks for evaluation criteria (see the table below).

Walking distance	Defects, scrap, rework, errors
Inventory levels	Energy levels (electricity, gas, coal, etc.)
Lead time or cycle time	Paperwork
Work balance (time at each workstation in a work cell)	Output (products completed, reports filed, attendance levels, etc.)
Changeover/setup/startup time	Utilities (water, sewer)

Key performance indicators (KPI) generally fall into categories like safety, quality, delivery, cost, productivity and people. These categories can also serve as evaluation criteria, provided they are specifically defined. In most cases C4 participants define their criteria based on the four criteria shown on the C4 worksheet: cost, ease to do, control and effectiveness, but each concern should warrant a specific review of important evaluation factors in light of company policies and priorities.

Cost: Cost is usually a major factor, but it can be measured in many different ways. To produce an unbiased analysis that yields the best result, a cost definition must be precise. In most cases, cost-evaluation criteria focus only on the implementation costs of a particular countermeasure, often overlooking other factors, including savings that might result from a that countermeasure. Savings are frequently included as an element of *effectiveness*, but they also should be treated as a direct offset to implementation costs. Consider the following when determining the true cost of a countermeasure:

- Does the countermeasure require new equipment? If so, at what exact cost?
- If no new equipment is required, what materials are needed to modify the existing process?
- Will the implementation require overtime? How much, by whom, and at what rate?

- Will the implementation require outside experts such as hardware or software consultants, technicians or installation specialists (including carpenters, electricians and plumbers)?
- How much will be spent on consumable supplies?
- How much and what type of savings (labor, material, space) will the countermeasure offer to offset the cost?

Recently, the authors helped a non-profit organization evaluate options for leasing office space. The organization's existing office, in a downtown tower, cost about $50,000 annually. (To keep the organization anonymous, we've changed all the numbers slightly.) In evaluating different office options, the only cost initially considered was the rent, reflected as cost per square foot. The existing office was nearly three times larger than needed. Other options were sized properly but required moderate custom remodeling to be suitable for the organization's use. The option eventually selected included an annual cost for rent of about $13,000, plus a one-time building charge of $9,500 and another $2,500 to move. Even at the combined cost of $25,000 for the first year, this option was a much better deal than renewing the lease for the existing office.

The lesson: If "cost" is an evaluation criterion, make sure it reflects not just the total cost of implementation but also the overall savings.

Ease to do: As an evaluation factor for anyone in the organization to use, ease to do is, well, easy. If one countermeasure is easier to implement than another, the first should receive a higher evaluation. What makes an implementation easy? Consider the following:

- Do team members have the skill and tools to complete the implementation?
- How long might it take to complete?
- Are other internal resources available and capable of implementing the countermeasure (maintenance, engineering, a continuous-improvement team, etc.)
- Are the materials required readily available?
- Can the implementation be completed during normal working hours, or will people have to work overtime? (This answer to this question is both an ease to do and a *cost* element.)

Control: Control is similar to *ease to do* but focuses instead on who has total control over the implementation, the team or someone else. If a countermeasure allows the team to have full control, including the freedom to make adjustments to the plan as each step is implemented, it should receive a higher score than, for example, a countermeasure that requires outside contractors to come in and build something. If detailed job orders have to be submitted to engineering or maintenance to complete without the full engagement of the team, or if management insists on reviewing and prioritizing every improvement project, the team loses control and the countermeasure receives a lower score. Consider the following:

- Who must approve the planned change?
- Does the team have the required expertise to do the job itself?
- Who is paying for the implementation?
- Can the team make changes to the plan without consulting management?

- What paperwork is required?
- Who must schedule the work to be done?

Effectiveness: This is the criterion that determines whether a countermeasure works as promised or not. Of course, it's impossible to be certain a countermeasure will work until it's in place. How, then, can effectiveness be used as a decision-making tool?

The best way to predict the effectiveness of a proposed countermeasure is through experimentation. When possible, the team should design a trial, control for random variation, implement the proposed solution on a very small scale, and then measure the results. Where it's not possible to conduct an actual trial, the team should attempt to gather data by simulating the solution with models. Often data such as distance travelled by staff to complete a job, or time saved to complete the work, is available from baseline data gathered during the *Concern* stage. In this case effectiveness can be calculated based on estimated differences gathered during an experiment or simulation.

When they think of experimentation, many people have a vision of a scientist in a laboratory, surrounded by test tubes. This is not necessarily the case. In most scenarios, experimentation starts with the trial-and-error approach we spoke rather disparagingly of earlier. The key difference in the case of experimentation, however, is that the trial is specifically designed to gather clearly defined pieces of information within a small scope. The design of the experiment, the planning, and the observation are all key differentiators. Consider the following:

- Does the countermeasure require less time than before?
- Does the countermeasure produce a better product (or service)?
- Will the result be consistent among different operators?
- Will it take less space or require less handling?
- Does it require fewer operators?

- Will it provide visible feedback for operators and managers?
- Will it require less material (lower inventory levels) and produce less scrap?
- Does it prevent people from making mistakes?

While all evaluation criteria are important, some are critical. In order to emphasize one or more criteria over others, we need to weight each criterion. Assigning weights to evaluation criteria also aligns the C4 process with company priorities. If a company is having financial difficulty, *cost* is likely to be the most important consideration. If the problem has public consequences or visibility, *effectiveness* is likely to be most important. If the problem involves sensitive technology or intellectual property, *control* may be paramount. When selecting evaluation criteria and assigning weights, teams need to critically think through the business environment.

There are several different ways to assign weights. Based on the circumstances, teams should pick *one* of the following strategies and then apply it to all criteria being evaluated for a particular problem:

- Assume all evaluation criteria are equal (no specific weights are defined):

    Ex: Cost = 25%; Ease to do = 25%; Control = 25%; Effectiveness = 25%

- Add a multiplier to the criteria that are more important:

    Ex: Cost = +3; Ease to do = 1; Control = 1; Effectiveness = +2

- Assign a specific percentage to each criterion so that the sum of all weights is 1:

    Ex: Cost = .30; Ease to do = .15; Control = .10; Effectiveness = .45

- Assign a value based on a 100-point scale. This approach is essentially the same as the previous technique but works better for those who prefer to work with whole numbers:

  Ex: Cost = 42; Ease to do = 15; Control = 21; Effectiveness = 22

We've just spent several pages describing evaluation criteria because we believe it's vital for teams to define their evaluation criteria before beginning to formulate a countermeasure. Why? Because defining criteria up front is the only way to guarantee an *unbiased* analysis of all options under consideration. Human nature makes most people very competitive, not to mention protective of their own ideas. When it's time to compare one countermeasure against another, having spelled out specific evaluation criteria helps prevent any one individual from manipulating the numbers so his or her preferred countermeasure "wins." In scientific experimentation, this objectivity is perhaps the most crucial aspect of the experimental design because, once discovered, any bias can have an adverse affect on both findings and on the personal relationships in a team. (And this type of bias, when it exists, is almost *always* discovered.) To avoid even the hint of bias, intended or not, teams need to take the time to define criteria up front, assigning weights based on company priorities.

Once evaluation criteria are defined, it's time to *formulate* the actual *Countermeasures*. As when looking for problems in the *Concern* stage and causes in the *Cause* stage, formulating workable countermeasures begins by brainstorming to identify every possible way to solve a problem. The best way to do this is to document *every* idea in a free-flowing, unstructured brainstorming session or to use a structured brainstorming technique like 6-3-3, described in Chapter 1.

If the problem is large or complex, it may be helpful to focus on a specific area (process flow, then material handling, then external logistics, etc.). Once the team has generated a large list of ideas, it should narrow this list using critical thinking, data collection and analysis—along with tools like the affinity diagram or multi-voting described earlier—to identify two or three feasible solution sets. (Most problems will require several countermeasure actions rather than one simple solution, thus the term "solution set.")

To define these two or three feasible solution sets, the team needs to involve all affected members. In other words, a problem-solving team cannot develop a solution for a problem in a work area without discussing the problem and resulting analysis with the people who do the work every day (unless, of course, the team doing the analysis *is* the actual work team).

Many problems will have smaller groups or even individuals assigned to complete the analysis or the evaluation of the proposed countermeasures. As information becomes available, it's important that the small group/individual share it on a regular basis with the rest of the work team members for their feedback.

The team should describe each countermeasure in detail, using whatever aids will make it clear to anyone who reviews the process (drawings, photos, spreadsheets, models, etc.) It's important to include action steps, people required and additional resources needed, as well as implementation costs. Most of this information will flow through team members' involvement and what they learn through experimentation. The authors recommend using a large flip chart or butcher paper to capture all the details of a countermeasure on one page. Some charts will be more detailed than others as the team identifies missing information it will need to gather.

Evaluate

The evaluation process consists of two distinct steps:

1. Evaluating each countermeasure against the selected evaluation

criteria, clearly identifying its pros and cons (see samples below).

2. Determining the best overall countermeasure by evaluating proposed countermeasures against each other using a decision matrix.

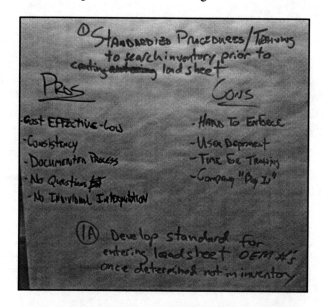

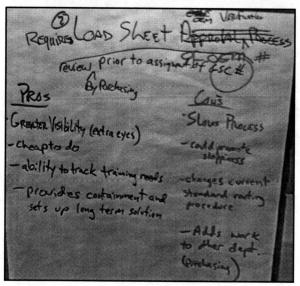

An example earlier in the chapter illustrated how the C4 process helped a non-profit organization evaluate options for a new office. Evaluation criteria included *cost, use of space, access for clients* and *political/ relationship implications*. In this case, cost was weighted at twice the value of each of the other three:

Cost = .4; Use of space = .2; Access for clients = .2; Pol./Rel. Implications = .2

Countermeasure #1	Countermeasure #2	Countermeasure #3	Countermeasure #4
----	----	----	----
Renew the lease; stay where you are (do nothing)	Close the office and consolidate with head-quarters (different city)	Rent smaller space in the same building	Move to new office space in a different building in the same city (offered by a partner organization)
Details: 3,500 sf; high floor, building carries the name of the organization, $15/sf.	*Details:* Organization was founded in current city. Some space (1,400 sf) is available in the HQ at no additional charge.	*Details:* 1,500 sf available on lower floor, building carries the name of the organization. Initial charge $15/sf but grows to $18/sf in 3 years.	*Details:* Partner organi-zation making 1,400 sf available and offering for $10/sf. City gov't facility with controlled access.
Action steps: Renew lease; business as usual.	*Action steps:* Plan the move – allocate space; secure packing/moving contracts; plan for client support during move. Move, unpack and resume operations.	*Action steps:* Secure new lease; plan the move; secure contracts; plan for client support. Move, unpack and resume operations.	*Action steps:* Secure new lease agreement; arrange for architect and builder to finish new space; plan move; plan for client support. Move, unpack and resume operations.
Pros: Easy for clients to find, no need to issue address changes etc. Retains good relationship with host city government.	Pros: Low cost except for one-time costs for modifications to existing space ($15,000) and moving costs ($15,000). Better use of space.	*Pros:* Cost lower ($24,750), space use more efficient; mod. costs moderate ($10,000); staying in host city maintains relationship with key parties. May be able to move without hiring moving contractor ($1,500).	Pros: Cost much lower ($14,000), with mod costs ($9,500) and low moving cost ($2,500); space use more efficient. Staying in the host city maintains or improves relationships; co-located.
Cons: Cost remains very high ($50,000); poor use of space (too much, paying for much more than we need).	*Cons:* Clients may be confused or worse with new location; space may be insufficient; likely to damage relationship with key funding source.	*Cons:* Not a prestigious office location (hard to find from elevator since it is around two corners). May require significant cleanup and customization.	*Cons:* May lose indepen-dent identity and potential clients might perceive the org. as a government entity. Possible conflicts of interest with government agency providing no-cost or low-cost space to a third party business entity. Harder location for clients/ members to find.

The Toolbox

DECISION MATRIX

Once every countermeasure had been evaluated on its own merits against the evaluation criteria, it was time to compare each against the others using a decision matrix.

The matrix used in this case is reproduced below. Evaluation criteria and weightings are listed across the top. Countermeasures are listed down the left-hand side.

Evaluation Criteria*	Cost	Use of Space		Access for Clients		Political Implications		Totals
Weights	0.40	0.20		0.20		0.20		
Countermeasure #1 - Stay where we are	1	1		5		4		
Countermeasure #2 - Consolidate in HQ city	4	4		3		1		
Countermeasure #3 - Smaller space in same building	3	4		3		4		
Countermeasure #4 - New host city office space	5	4		2		4		

*High score is better for all categories

The chart was completed by comparing the four countermeasure options based on the four criteria of *cost, use of space, access for clients* and *political/relationship implications.*

The first comparison was based on *cost.*

- At $50,000 for annual rent, Countermeasure #1 was significantly more costly than the other three; thus it received the lowest score (1).

- The least expensive option was Countermeasure #4 at $26,000; it received the highest score (5).

- Countermeasure #2 was next lowest and received a score of 4.

- Countermeasure #3, being more expensive than Countermeasure #2 but still considerably lower than Countermeasure #1, received a score of 3.

- The next criterion, weighted at .2 or 20 percent, was based on *use of space.*
- Countermeasure #1 again scored lowest, since it is too much space for the organization.
- All three of the others were virtually the same size and all received the score of 4. None of the spaces was perfect so none received a 5. In the absence of accurate data, this process still contains some subjectivity. For example, if the organization had known that its optimal space requirement was 1,500 sf, it could have compared this requirement to the actual square footage of each of the proposed countermeasures and rated the results as follows:

Countermeasure #1	3,500 sf	Rated: 2
Countermeasure #2	1,320 sf	Rated: 3
Countermeasure #3	1,460 sf	Rated: 4
Countermeasure #4	1,510 sf	Rated: 5

Since the intention is to minimize potential for bias in the evaluation, the more hard data available, the more effective the selected countermeasure is likely to be.

The third criterion, again weighted at .2 or 20 percent, was based on *access for clients.* This measurement was meant to assess how easy it would be for the organization's existing clients to find them; thus, the easier for a client to find the office, the higher the score. Clients were familiar with the existing location, so clearly the current office location received the highest score (5). If the organization moved downstairs in the same building or to an entirely new city, everyone felt clients would be equally confused and have trouble finding the office. Thus Countermeasures #3 and #4 each received a mid-value score of 3. Countermeasure #4—a new office building in the same city—received the lowest score because it was a new government building with a security check station that clients would have to navigate to reach the office. Since this space would be the most troublesome for clients to access, it was rated a 2.

The final criterion considered *political and relationship implications* associated with the move. The current host city provided funding for the organization and was very interested in keeping its offices in the city. In this case, moving to another city (Countermeasure #2) was the least-preferred option, so it received a score of 1. Choosing to remain in the city, regardless of address, had the same impact politically. Thus the other three options received a score of 4.

To calculate a total score, each individual score was multiplied by the weight of the evaluation factor with which it was associated. For example, the score under *cost* for Countermeasure #3 is 3; the weight for this factor is .40.

Cost: score of 3 x weight of .40 = adjusted score of 1.2

The *use-of-space* score was 4, while the weight for this criterion was .2, resulting in an adjusted score for use of space of .8, and so forth. Totaling the adjusted scores for a given countermeasure generates a total score for that option. In this case, Countermeasure #4, the option the organization chose to implement, received the highest score (4.0) of those considered.

Countermeasure #4: cost (2) + use of space (.8) + access (.4) + politics (.8) = 4.0

Evaluation Criteria*	Cost		Use of Space		Access for Clients		Political Implications		Totals
Weights	0.40		0.20		0.20		0.20		
Countermeasure #1 - Stay where we are	1	0.4	1	0.2	5	1.0	4	0.8	2.40
Countermeasure #2 - Consolidate in HQ city	4	1.6	4	0.8	3	0.6	1	0.2	3.20
Countermeasure #3 - Smaller space in same building	3	1.2	4	0.8	3	0.6	4	0.8	3.40
Countermeasure #4 - New host city office space	5	2	4	0.8	2	0.4	4	0.8	4.0

*High score is better for all categories

There's no question the decision matrix is a useful tool. Still, given the simple scores in the boxes, it can be challenging even for an entire team to control for bias. Imagine, therefore, how easy it would be for a single individual to manipulate the weightings and the scores so the matrix reflected more favorably on his or her preferred countermeasure.

Often, the team doing the evaluation lacks the authority to decide which countermeasure to implement. Especially in the case of capital expenditures or structural changes to the facilities, senior leaders are likely to ask a team do the analysis and then prepare a recommendation upon which management can base a decision. When a decision matrix is properly completed without bias, the decision-making process should be straightforward. The team makes its presentation regarding the definition of all countermeasures, along with an explanation of the evaluation criteria, the weighting used, and how each countermeasure was evaluated. A decision matrix such as the one above shows the final result.

Provided the team has done its homework and is working with the level of detail leadership expects, this type of quantitative analysis is very difficult to argue with. It's true the decision-maker may choose to throw out everything the team has done and go with a completely different solution. That's his or her prerogative as the big chief, but the responsibility for the decision rests on his shoulders as well.

Since leaders are responsible for teaching the four stages of C4 to the workforce, it's important they stay engaged with the team throughout the process to be available for additional coaching or advice as necessary. On the other hand, they should not become so involved they're perceived by the team as taking over or micromanaging. Challenging, thoughtful questions that probe the team's thought processes or enhance its skills in data collection and/or analysis are fair game. Workers should expect this type of questioning from servant leaders at every level.

Plan

The fourth step in the five-step process of developing countermeasures is to prepare a detailed implementation plan for the countermeasure selected under the *evaluate* step above. Here's the path to follow:

- Define precise action steps. The clearer the instructions the better.

- Specifically identify who, what, where and when for each action step

- Define measurements of success, including how to know when the implementation is complete. (This step requires that the team review baseline measures to compare the results of the countermeasure with the original state.)

Use the Countermeasure: Implementation Plan space on the C4 worksheet to record the action plan as well as the status at different milestones as the implementation progresses.

Countermeasure: Implementation Plan		Develop an implementation schedule recording status and results as: 0 = Acceptable; Δ = Needs improvement; x = Poor												
Implementation Steps	Who's responsible													Date complete

A successful implementation must be fast and forceful. If it drags on and on, people find more and more reasons not to support it or to finish the plan. Once the plan is complete, it's important to set an implementation date in the *near* future or to begin immediately. Muster all the resources necessary to finish. Set a hard deadline for process and system changes (usually within five days). Set a hard date (usually within six weeks) for all team members/associates/employees to reach the new performance standard that goes with the new process.

Implement

As simple as it sounds, far too many groups/teams/individuals/ companies get to this point and then fail miserably to execute the plan. Whether the problem is simple or complex, groups regularly complete all kinds of detailed plans but never execute them. Busy work schedules, combined with a lack of leadership, tend to be the biggest culprits in most lack-of-execution scenarios. In other words, a company puts a team together to begin solving a problem, but company leadership fails to make explicit the fact that the work of the team *supersedes* the work of the individual. If this priority is not made crystal clear, people often get so caught up in their individual work assignments that their work with the team is viewed as "extra." Extra work almost never assumes the priority of primary work. When short on time, therefore, most people complete work in their regular job description rather than tackle the extra stuff. After all, that's what they're getting paid for, right?

Overcoming this natural human inclination is the work of leaders. For the C4 process—or any process involving long-term work improvement—to succeed, everyone, leaders included, must view problem solving as an integral piece of his or her work. In today's competitive market, companies no longer have the luxury of allowing one person to point out a problem and then wait for someone else to solve it. All organizations must become *learning organizations*. The key to developing a learning organization is creating a structure for problem solving where leaders set the expectation that everything the organization does needs to be done better: more efficiently, more easily, less wastefully, and at a lower cost. Doing whatever it takes to create and sustain a learning organization should be part of every leader's evaluation plan. If the performance of a company's leaders is not evaluated based on the requirements of problem solving (learning), there will be no progress.

While executing the implementation plan quickly and thoroughly, it's important the team continue to work together, one step at a time, until the task is complete. The status of the implementation needs to be communicated frequently (at least daily) to team members, leaders and those associated with adjacent processes. When there is a need to deviate from the plan, let the entire team know immediately and then *stop*! Get together—right away—to solve the new problem, adjust the plan and keep pushing. Never abandon the countermeasure and return to the way it was before.

Whenever change occurs, there are always plenty of naysayers to insist the solution won't work. If the team has followed the C4 process and done its analysis properly, however, the solution *will* work once the implementation is complete. It may take a little while for everyone to reach the new standard associated with the solution, but eventually it will work for nearly everyone. Therefore, it's important to *always go forward*, adapting as necessary and keeping the owners of the process fully engaged with the implementation team.

C4 Worksheet Example: The StrikeFighter

During the StrikeFighter simulation, the overall problem was that only 4 aircraft were delivered when 15 were due. During the first stage of the C4 process, one group broke the problem into several concerns, listing, in order of priority: communication and collaboration, picking parts in the warehouse, delivering parts to workstations, process assembly steps, and quality.

The team stated the main problem or *Concern* as "teams developed solutions without considering the needs of the enterprise" and set a goal of "within 90 minutes, develop an effective communication and transportation system that works for everyone." During the *Cause* stage, the team determined the root cause was, "We didn't choose a leader or facilitator to organize planning for the enterprise."

Countermeasures began with evaluation criteria, and the team consistently picked implementation cost. Although cost was probably not a significant factor for this particular problem, it was likely to be for many of the other countermeasures the team needed to develop to succeed: ease to implement (including time to implement), control over the implementation, and expected effectiveness.

To specifically address the root cause, the team needed several different approaches, so they brainstormed the following list:

- Appoint a leader
- Joint leadership among the four teams
- Seek a volunteer to lead
- Ask outside staff to lead/facilitate
- Just roll with what we have . . . we know what we need

Team members decided the last option was invalid. They knew they needed a leader to direct their activities, so rolling with what they had was unlikely to be successful. They could ask outside staff to lead, but since such a leader would not have experienced what the team had experienced, his or her effectiveness would be weak at best. This option was also rejected as a feasible alternative. The other three approaches were listed as Countermeasures 1, 2 and 3 and designated for further evaluation.

Countermeasure 1 – Appoint a Leader

In this case, the idea was to select a leader who could see how the whole system fit together, someone who had been an active participant in the simulation and shared ideas about building StrikeFighters. The team considered appointing this individual from the prime contractor team since he or she may already have established limited relationships with other teams in the course of earlier simulation rounds.

Pros: The countermeasure should be relatively easy and quick to implement. The team has full control over the decision. It should be an effective solution provided a competent leader is chosen.

Cons: Appointing someone who may not welcome the responsibility runs the risk that the leader will disengage and not give the team the direction it needs.

Countermeasure 2 – Joint Leadership Among the Four Teams

In this scenario, a group of four leaders, one from each team, would work together as equals, meeting frequently to assign people to projects designed to solve other problems affecting the system.

Pros: Since all four teams will be working together, leaders are likely to be more fully engaged in a spirit of system-wide cooperation.

Cons: Decisions are likely to take longer. Even among this group of equals, someone will have to step up and call meetings, lead discussions, facilitate.

Countermeasure 3 – Seek a Volunteer to Lead

This scenario invites a volunteer from the group to serve as the enterprise leader. If more than one person volunteers, the group would hold an election.

Pros: A leader selected through this method is likely to want the job. The countermeasure should be easy to implement.

Cons: People may want the job for the wrong reasons. Finding a leader could take longer if it becomes necessary to hold an election. A volunteer may lack leadership or other skills the group needs.

The decision matrix used to evaluate these three countermeasures is shown below.

Countermeasures	Brainstorm countermeasures and evaluate each potential solution, ranking them with 5 being best and 1 being worst. You may weight-load the categories according to company priorities.							
Countermeasure		Cost	Ease to do		Control		Effectiveness (savings or performance)		Total
Weights		0.0	0.4		0.2		0.4		
Countermeasure 1 – Appoint a leader			5	2.0	5	1.0	3	1.2	4.2
Countermeasure 2 – Group leadership			2	0.8	3	0.6	5	2.0	3.4
Countermeasure 3 – Solicit volunteer			3	1.2	2	0.4	1	0.4	2.0

Selected Countermeasure (s):

Short Term: Instructor facilitated discussion

Long Term: C/M 1 - Engage the group in a brief discussion focusing on the four current team leaders. As

Selection rationale: we learn more about the strengths of individual team leaders and team members, we will be

able to decide who would make the best group leader, and ask that person to step up and take

the job.

Based on the results, the solution chosen was to appoint a leader.

In order to select that individual, the group planned to engage in a brief discussion, focusing on the four current team leaders. As members learned more about the strengths of individual team leaders and other team members, they felt they'd be able to decide who would make the best group leader and then ask that person to step up and take the job.

Countermeasure: Implementation Plan		Develop an implementation schedule recording status and results as: O = Acceptable; Δ = Needs improvement; x = Poor												
Implementation Steps	Who's responsible	11:30	12:00	12:30	1:00	1:30	2:00	2:30	3:00	3:30	4:00	4:30	5:00	Date complete
Appoint group leader	Group	O												
Assign joint teams for problems	Group leader		O											
Present recommended C/Ms	Team leaders				O									
Implement selected C/Ms	Teams					O								
Final prep for simulation run	Teams							O						

Following this appointment, groups are remarkably consistent in their willingness to step up to responsibilities and help out where needed.

The problem of selecting a group leader doesn't necessarily take a long time to solve and, let's face it, it's hardly the meat of what needs to be addressed. Solving the other problems identified—picking and delivering parts, reworking the flow of assembly, and balancing the work—is much more likely to contribute to success than simply appointing a group leader. On the other hand, without a leader, most teams develop independent solutions *even after the instructor points out the critical requirement of joint solutions.*

During past simulations, once a group leader was selected, he or she formed problem-solving teams composed of members from each working team. For each of the remaining problem sets, these new teams did a root cause analysis, developed countermeasures and made recommendations to the entire group for action. (Here the authors deliberately chose to showcase the leadership problem—rather than one of the other three—to avoid presenting solutions that could be used by future groups who may be completing the simulation.)

C4 Worksheet Example: Plywood Panels

The group working on the problem of out-of-square plywood panels focused on the smaller, solvable problem of "uneven air pressure on hold-down wheels." It determined that the root *Causes* of the uneven pressure were (1) the equipment required many adjustments in many places and (2) operators lacked standardized work for the saw.

As in the StrikeFighter example above, *Countermeasure* formulation for this problem began by defining the evaluation criteria. The worksheet used is shown here.

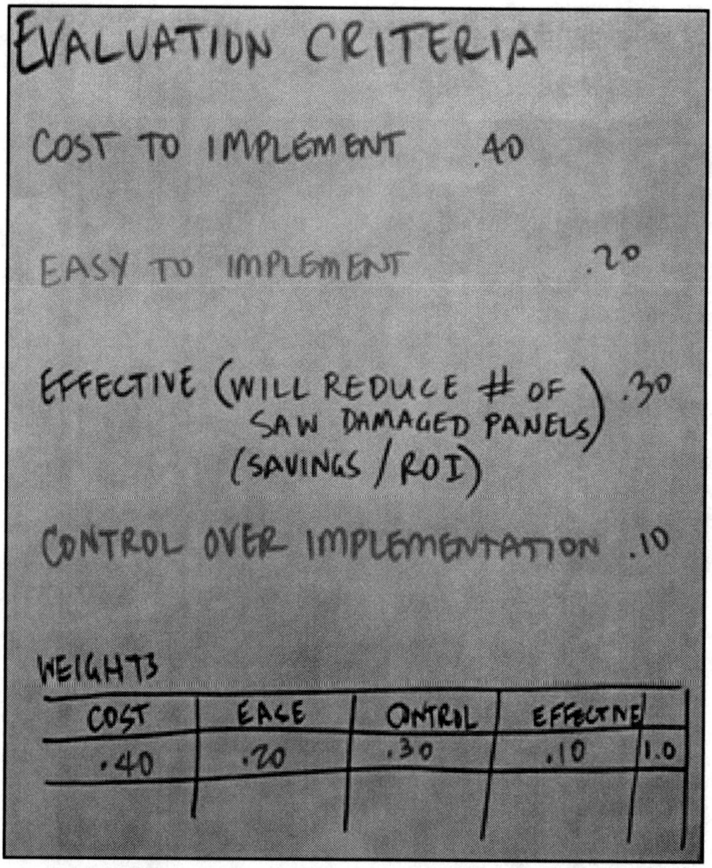

EVALUATION CRITERIA

COST TO IMPLEMENT .40

EASY TO IMPLEMENT .20

EFFECTIVE (WILL REDUCE # OF SAW DAMAGED PANELS) .30
(SAVINGS / ROI)

CONTROL OVER IMPLEMENTATION .10

WEIGHTS

COST	EASE	CONTRL	EFFECTNE	
.40	.20	.30	.10	1.0

The group decided to employ the four standard C4 evaluation criteria: *cost, ease-to-do, control* and *effectiveness,* then weighted each as shown.

- Cost: .40
- Ease to do (in this case, easy to implement): .20
- Control (over implementation): .30
- Effectiveness (defined as "will reduce # of saw-damaged panels," savings, and return on investment [ROI]): .10

With its evaluation criteria defined, the group then brainstormed a list of possible solutions. On a flip chart with the root cause written at the top, a scribe recorded everything each team member said.

- 1 gauge, not 2 for adjustment
- Connect to auto setup

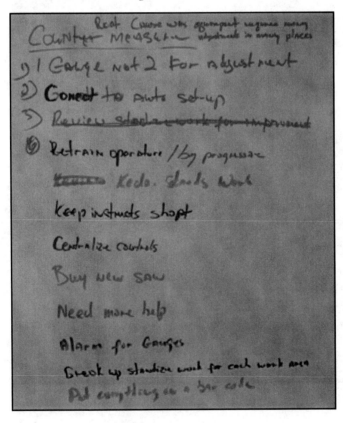

- Review standardized work for improvement
- Retrain operators / by Progressive (the saw manufacturer)
- Redo standardized work
- Keep instructions short
- Centralize controls
- Buy [a] new saw
- Need more help
- Alarm for gauges
- Break up standardized work for each work area
- Put everything as a bar code

Through consensus, the group settled on four countermeasures, which it then defined and evaluated against the cost, ease of implementation, control and effectiveness criteria (see the table below).

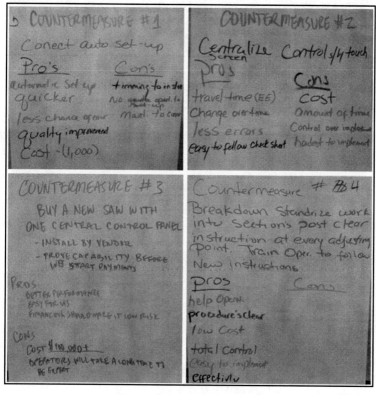

Countermeasure 1 ---- Connect to an automatic setup	Countermeasure 2 ---- Centralize the control panel with a touch screen	Countermeasure 3 ---- Buy a new saw	Countermeasure 4 ---- Break down standardized work for every adjustment point
Details: Maintenance crew can build and program an automatic setup function to relieve operators from having to make separate adjustments for each area.	*Details:* Buy a touch screen control panel to make all adjustments at one spot.	*Details:* New saw with one central control panel; installed by vendor; prove capability before we start payments.	*Details:* New standardized work broken down into sections posting clear instructions at every adjusting point. Train operators to follow new instructions.
Pros: Automatic setup. Quicker; less chance for operator error; quality improvement; low cost ($1,000).	*Pros:* Employee travel time reduced; reduce overtime; fewer errors; easy to follow cheat sheet.	*Pros:* Better performance; easy for us; financing should make it lower risk.	*Pros:* Should help operators; will make procedures much clearer; lowest cost; total control; easy to implement; will be more effective.
Cons: Timing to install (may take too long); no guarantee that operators will use the auto setup; new maintenance requirements for the setup.	*Cons:* Higher cost; may take longer time to install; little control over the implementation; may be hardest to implement.	*Cons:* High cost (>$100,000); may take operators a long time to become experts on a new saw.	*Cons:* Doesn't save any operator travel distance.

After completing its evaluation, the team constructed a decision matrix (shown below).

DECISION MATRIX

EVAL CRITERIA WEIGHTS	COST .40		EASE .20		CONTROL .10		EFFECTIVE .30		TOTALS 1.0
CM1 CONNECT TO AUTO SET UP	4	1.6	4	.8	4	.4	4	1.2	4.0
CM2 CENTRALIZE CONTROLS @ TOUCH SCREEN	3	1.2	2	.4	3	.3	3	.9	2.8
CM3 BUY NEW SAW	1	.4	1	.2	1	.1	5	1.5	2.2
CM4 STD WK	5	2.0	5	1.0	5	.5	3	.9	4.4

The best option is clearly Countermeasure 4: update the standardized work. The scores also reflected positively on Countermeasure 1: connect to an automatic setup system. After consulting with its maintenance team members, the team decided to build the automatic setup system in house, then tailor the standardized work to the automatic setup.

To implement these countermeasures, the team developed a plan with its technicians to have a test board developed within four weeks. Testing would take place over the following four weeks, after which there would be a scheduled shutdown to put the automatic setup system in place. The team would begin developing the standardized work soon after testing started and planned to finish the week before implementation so all operators could be trained prior to full implementation.

Portions of the C4 worksheet reflecting the four countermeasures considered, along with details of the implementation plan for those selected, are shown below.

Countermeasures — Brainstorm countermeasures and evaluate each potential solution, ranking them with 5 being best and 1 being worst. You may weight-load the categories according to company priorities.

Countermeasure	Cost		Ease to do		Control		Effectiveness		Total
Weights	0.4		0.2		0.1		0.3 (performance)		
Countermeasure 1 – Connect to Auto setup	4	1.6	4	0.8	4	0.4	4	1.2	4.0
Countermeasure 2 – Central touch screen	3	1.2	2	0.4	3	0.3	3	0.9	2.8
Countermeasure 3 – Buy new saw	1	0.4	1	0.2	1	0.1	5	1.5	2.2
Countermeasure 4 – Standardized work	5	2.0	5	1.0	5	0.5	3	0.9	4.4

Selected Countermeasure (s):

Short Term: Enforce improved standardized work

Long Term: C/M 1 – Create and install Automatic setup. Develop new standardized work and train

Selection rationale: operators to meet the new standard.

Countermeasure: Implementation Plan — Develop an implementation schedule recording status and results as: 0 = Acceptable; Δ = Needs improvement; x = Poor

Implementation Steps	Who's responsible	2/14	2/28	3/15	3/30	4/15	4/30	5/15	5/30	6/15	6/30	7/15	7/30	Date complete
Rework current std work	Team leader	O												
Develop test panel	Maintenance/Engr		O											
Testing	CI Team/Maint/Engr			O										
Develop new std work	CI Team w/TL					O								
Final implementation of panel	CI Team/Maint/Engr								O					
All operators proficient in SW	Team leader											O		

Once the solution was implemented, the team entered the final stage of the C4 process, *Confirm*. This stage is discussed at length in the following chapter.

CHAPTER 6

Confirm: Embedding Learning

Previous chapters discussed the first three elements of the C4 process:

- Accurately articulating a *Concern*;
- Deliberately determining the root *Cause(s)*; and
- Carefully crafting and aggressively implementing one or more *Countermeasures*.

This chapter explores the *Confirm* stage, or the role of continuous improvement. Problem solving and continuous improvement are two sides of the same coin, and both suffer from the consequences of failure to follow up. Without the *Confirm* piece of the process, it's easy to backslide, thus losing gains achieved from implementing a *Countermeasure*.

The *Confirm* stage of C4 is at the heart of a learning organization. It's designed to embed new lessons in the workplace by following these three key steps:

- Standardize;
- Track results; and
- Reflect.

The combination of these actions, when executed with discipline, will ensure complete implementation of *Countermeasures* and achieve successful results, whether such results are corrections to problems or improvements to processes.

Standardize

The end result of the C4 process is new standardized work. Standardized work is not simply a procedure or work instruction. Rather, it involves a deep analysis of the work required at a workstation, work center or office, or the work of leaders. In fact, when attempting to create a new culture within an organization, the development and use of standardized work is *the* critical element.

The details of creating standardized work are beyond the scope of this book, but here are some facts to consider:

- The primary goal of standardized work is to understand the work required and design a safe and effective workplace in which to complete it;
- The analysis piece of building standardized work will expose best practices and improvement opportunities; and
- Analysis allows designers to build in safety and quality requirements, cap inventory levels (of either physical materials or virtual information), and measure productivity.

Locking in the agreed-upon standard, training everyone in proper work techniques, and then enforcing the standard by insisting everyone do the work the same way, has several benefits for both the organization and the workers. When everyone follows the standardized work, variability in the process is reduced, resulting in better quality, reliability and predictability. When people complete a work function the same way each time, over time they get better at it. Their skills improve; more importantly, their self-efficacy improves as well.

Self-efficacy is a judgment people make—based on their perceptions of what's going on in the workplace and the information available to them—about their ability to perform a particular task or to have control over a particular situation. It's a special type of work-related *confidence*. Workers with high self-efficacy are more likely to try new things related to their work; to take steps to improve their work; and to persist after failures. Think how much farther a company could go on the continuous-improvement journey if the entire workforce had high self-efficacy, if everyone tried new things to make the workplace better and, when something failed, tried again and again to make it right?

Self-efficacy flows from success. Repeated success leads to mastery or expertise. The better someone is at a particular task, the higher his or her confidence about performing that task. Standardized work is the only tool that can build self-efficacy, because it assures repeated success. When standardized work is combined with a team-based work environment in which people both learn from and coach each other, workers develop strong feelings of control over their destiny and are willing to take reasonable risks with new ideas. All their attempts will not succeed, but high self-efficacy compels them to keep trying. This willingness to try again—and again—is *exactly* what's needed to create and sustain a continuous-improvement and problem-solving culture within today's organizations.

Because standardized work means everyone is doing the work the same way, problems related to the work are more likely to become evident. A learning organization does not hide from problems; it embraces them. In fact, in an ideal scenario problems are not only visible, they're also painful. Why should problems be painful? Because something that hurts gets fixed faster than something that doesn't hurt. It's just human nature.

To those in a mature organization, standardized work seems extremely dynamic, with hundreds if not thousands of changes made by the workforce daily. For those just beginning this improvement journey, the first step is to define the standardized work through detailed job analysis. *This step could take up to several weeks.*

When the standardized work is being defined, every operator involved in the work needs to be involved in the process to some degree. However, there are two reasons why operators cannot prepare standardized work for their own work areas:

1. They have to work. Few companies have the luxury to stop working for several days to document the standardized work, let alone for several weeks more to ensure operators reach the required skill level.

2. In most cases, operators don't acknowledge the benefit to be derived from standardized work and thus are more likely to document the way a favorite coworker does the job rather than completing the proper analysis. Not only does this approach rarely elicit the most effective way to accomplish the task at hand, it also fails to set challenging new standards.

Once all operators have developed sufficient skill and are consistently meeting the new standard, they will almost always begin finding better ways to do the work. Some people may see better ways immediately. Before implementing their new idea, these workers should be encouraged to help the rest of the team reach the required skill level. If leaders responsible for documenting the standardized work have truly engaged the workforce in the process, good ideas will begin to emerge even during the initial learning and documentation period. Until everyone reaches the standard, however, the standardized work must be set in stone. Afterward, it should be flexible enough to change every hour.

While teams are learning the standardized work, leaders need to work on defining a standard process for making changes to the standardized work. As people come up with ideas to make the standardized work better, organizations must be prepared to teach the proper way to make these changes quickly, without risks to safety, quality, delivery, cost or morale.

The C4 process is the perfect tool for making these changes. When a worker has a new idea, the first step toward implementing that idea is to do a quick but thorough analysis of it with the help of a coach. This interaction facilitates the critical thinking step discussed in Chapter 3 (who, what, when, where, how). The next steps are to set the new target (*Concern*), identify barriers to accomplishing it (*Cause*), redefine the process to attain the new target (*Countermeasure*), and update and teach the new standard (*Confirm*).

There's space on the C4 worksheet to record the location of the standardized work documentation set so people can trace the history of the standardized work related to that particular process.

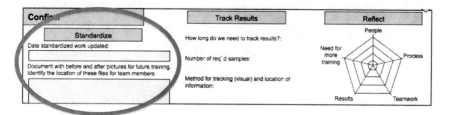

To summarize:

- The outcome of the C4 process is a new set of standardized work.
- Standardized work should be used to teach everyone the new performance standard. (Applying job-instruction techniques from the Training Within Industry [TWI] program is one way to guarantee great learning results.)
- When standardized work is enforced, operators build mastery and self-efficacy.
- The C4 process also can be used to standardize the process for making changes to the standardized work.

Track Results

Tracking results begins in the *Concern* stage with the selection of appropriate metrics. Chapter 3 included a list of several things to measure; they're listed again here.

Walking distance	Defects, scrap, rework, errors
Inventory levels	Energy levels (electricity, gas, coal, etc.)
Lead time or cycle time	Paperwork
Work balance (time at each workstation in a work cell)	Output (products completed, reports filed, attendance levels, etc.)
Changeover/setup/startup time	Utilities (water, sewer)

When tailored with specific points of measurement (walking distance in feet per cycle; pages of paperwork printed per day, etc.), these metrics are useful benchmarks to help determine the effectiveness of short-term *Countermeasures* applied in order to keep people working. They're also helpful when evaluating different long-term *Countermeasures* to select the best option. During the *Confirm* stage, they are used to monitor key indicators over a defined period to ensure selected *Countermeasures* are permanently effective.

Sometimes a new metric serves only to validate an improvement, such as a reduction in floor space or walking distance for an operator. At other times selected metrics may require high-frequency observation, then gradually be checked less often until monitoring is no longer necessary. This scenario is often the case for concerns targeting cycle time reductions or productive output. When operators are learning the new processes, it may be appropriate to measure every cycle. Later, frequencies can drop to daily measurement, then weekly or monthly spot checks, until finally there is no longer a need to measure at all.

In still other cases, the new metrics become part of the overall daily management system and will be tracked permanently. These types of measurements are true key performance indicators, able to provide immediate feedback when a condition is out of standard. As such, they should clearly indicate when there are violations of standardized work. For example, a metric such as first-pass yield, normally considered a quality metric, also serves as a conformance-to-standardized-work metric. If the standardized work has been properly prepared, following it should yield a quality result. Therefore, if defects or errors occur, it is reasonable to assume someone failed to follow the standardized work. Discovering the identity of this individual helps to detect problems with the way the work has been prepared and documented. Once again, the reason for identifying problems is not to demand one person "do it right" but to ensure everyone "does it better."

On occasion, particularly when implementing a *Countermeasure* that targets an improvement in product quality, results need to be tracked long enough to generate statistical confidence that the improvement is the result of the *Countermeasure* and not a random occurrence. In such instances, it's important to calculate the sample size for the confidence required: 95 percent, 99 percent or, for a Six Sigma result, 3.4 defective parts per million. If what's needed is a sample of 100 units and it's possible to collect one sample per day, then results must be tracked for 100 days. If the sample needs to be 20,000 units but it's possible to collect 1,000 samples per day, results will have to be tracked for only 20 days. Details of these statistics are beyond the scope of this book, but help is available from local Six Sigma Black Belts or from *The Black Belt Memory Jogger: A Pocket Guide for Six Sigma Success*, published by GOAL/QPC.

If the results ever indicate the *Countermeasure* has failed, the team should begin again at the *Concern* stage and reanalyze the problem using current information.

The C4 worksheet includes space to record tracking plans.

Reflect

Arguably the most important activity in the C4 process is reflection. Reflection reinforces learning. Critically thinking through every step of the process reveals strengths and weaknesses of the C4 process itself as well as information about how a team has applied that process when solving a real problem. When reflecting on past successes (or failures), it's important to consider not only the results achieved but also the impact of those results on various stakeholders.

Although the Confirm block is the only spot on the C4 worksheet that demands a team engage in reflection, reflection should occur repeatedly through the process. Many groups have found it helpful to engage in a brief after-action review of activities and results at the end of each "C"— *Concern, Cause,* and *Countermeasure.* A few questions to ask during a period of reflection include:

- Did we have the right people on the team for this problem?
- Did we have the right amount of support from management?
- Did we engage everyone on the team? Did we develop as a team through this activity?
- Did everyone on the team participate in each stage of the C4 process?
- Did the team engage process owners in the process?
- Did the team stick to the process, or did it take a shortcut

somewhere? Why? Where? What would be different if a shortcut had not been taken?

- What problems did the team encounter when completing the analysis during each stage of the process?
- Did the team have access to the right data in the right format?

This list is not meant to be exhaustive, but asking these questions offers a strong foundation for discussion. The idea is to set aside at least 90 minutes to reflect on every step of the process. Members should challenge their thinking by considering the perspectives of different groups—operators, managers, those who work on different shifts, customers.

The radar chart at the bottom of the C4 worksheet provides space to guide the team's reflection activity as it considers the following topics: *people, process, teamwork, results* and *need for more training*. For each process under review, teams can add topics or remove any that may not apply.

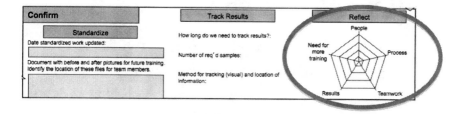

Based on answers to the guiding questions listed above, the team scores its performance in each of the five topic areas by placing dots on the chart. The higher the score, the closer the dots will be to the outside of the chart.

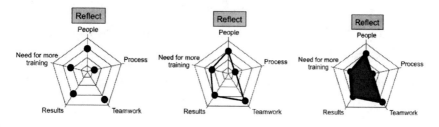

For example, if the team believes it had the perfect combination of *people* for a particular effort, the *people* dot would be on the outer edge of the chart. If none of the members was right for the task, the dot would be in the center. The same holds true for *process, teamwork* and achieving *results.*

The *need-for-more-training* topic can be trickier. If members think the problem provided a sufficient challenge to thoroughly develop their skills in problem solving, they would score this element higher than if the problem was less taxing or did not challenge them enough.

Once a team has scored each of the elements, it's time to connect the dots and color in the defined area. A chart that's completely colored in—in other words, every dot was at the outside edge—reflects a perfect score. If team members are honest, there will never be a perfect score, but teams that do well may choose to tackle other, more challenging problems, provided they have management support to do so.

C4 Worksheet Example: The StrikeFighter

At the beginning of the StrikeFighter simulation, participants were given a rough set of standardized work, which was held by each team leader. They tracked results only until the end of the next simulation round. Reflection, however, encompassed the team's experience for the whole simulation as well as for the workshop of which the simulation was a part.

As reflected on the *people* score, the group whose experience is depicted below thought the team needed members with more diverse experience. Members also agreed they failed to follow the recommended *process* during the *Countermeasure* stage and thus scored themselves accordingly. On the other hand, they felt they'd come together as a *team* very well. They also gave themselves a high score for *results* because they'd delivered all 15 aircraft. However, because they took more than the allotted 14 minutes to deliver all 15, they should have lowered their score a little. Finally, they agreed they could use additional *training*.

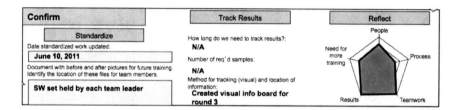

C4 Worksheet Example: Plywood Panels

The team working on this issue was pulled together specifically for problem-solving training. Members selected a problem together and then worked together to complete the detailed analysis described in earlier chapters. However, they were unable to fully implement the *Countermeasure* they recommended. Individually, members made headway on the standardized work but not on the central touch-screen control panel recommended to the organization. The Reflect graph below echos this performance. The team did not believe it had the right *people*, since it was unable to see the implementation plan through to completion. Scores for *process, results* and *need for more training* demonstrate this as well. Members did feel they came together as a team pretty well, given the short amount of time they were together.

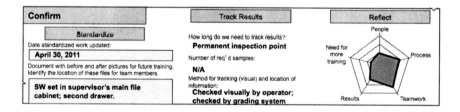

C4 is a process for everyone in the organization. Structured problem solving requires repeated application to take root and be effective. Like any skill, people have to do it many times to achieve mastery.

When the team learns, ideally the organization learns as well. Thus reflection should include discussions of where else in the enterprise lessons learned might apply, along with how to share these lessons with key people. Organizations need to create systems and structures that help problem-solving and continuous-improvement teams publicize their discoveries. These structures should include visual cues to let everyone know the status of ongoing projects, as well as ways to communicate the many daily improvement ideas that bubble up through an organization.

Handling these daily ideas—always a challenge—is the topic of the next chapter.

C-4 Worksheet

Concern – Cause – Countermeasure – Confirm

Theme: Delivery - Delivered 4 StrikeFighters when 15 were due
Ultimate goal: Deliver 15 perfect StrikeFighters on time
Date assigned: 3/29/2011

Team Member: _____ Shift: ___
Team Leader: _____ Shift: ___
C-4 Coach: _____ Shift: ___

Concern: Understand the current situation

Use charts, diagrams, or photos whenever possible to describe the solution.

Who discovered this problem? Gather findings from any previous studies of this problem area. Prime contractor. No previous studies available.

Describe what is happening to indicate a problem: Aircraft weren't ready when the customer came to pick them up. Everyone was waiting for materials.

Describe the deal condition. What standard is involved if any? We would deliver each aircraft, perfectly finished, just in time for delivery, with no excess materials

When does this problem occur? How frequently? (What are your angry clouds?) Aircraft are due 1 per minute beginning at minute 16. We could not build 1 per minute.

What is this problem costing the organization? $137,400,000 on the 2.5 year contract.

Break down the target problem. List the contributing problems below, sorting them by category. Attach an affinity diagram.

Current State Value Stream or Process Map. Summarize here and indicate where others can find fully detailed map.

VSM pictures and details are in the file cabinet in the quality manager's office.

What are the key problem areas on the map? Waiting for parts. Too much work in some work cells, not enough in others. Truck drivers could not find parts

Concern: Write your problem and goal statement

What do you want to accomplish? Be concise but as specific as possible. Make a statement of effort (OEE is considerably low – and 46% when standard is 67%) and then set an aggressive goal related to the Ultimate goal (Example: Decrease cycle time by 8 seconds by January) or a question to be answered (How do we get all team members trained on new systems by the end of the year?).

Problem: Teams developed solutions without considering the needs of the enterprise

Goal: Within 90 minutes, develop an effective communication and transportation system that works for everyone

Cause: Analysis

Brainstorm and organize potential causes or obstacles using the Fishbone diagram, stem-and-leaf diagram or other organizing tool. Write the causes of the problem or obstacles to improvement in the space provided always verifying that what you record is an actual CAUSE of the problem.

Priority Causes	What else?	Who else?	When?	Evaluation	Rank order
Did not do problem solving – no planning	Tools for planning – C4	No one	Before next round	Which will have greater impact	2
No leader to coordinate among teams	Nothing	No one	Before next round	Which will have greater impact	1

Cause: 5 Why Analysis

Problem: Did not do Problem Solving/No planning
Why? Working to solve our own problems
Why? No one facilitated the problem solving
Why? We didn't choose a leader or facilitator
Why?

Problem: No leader to coordinate among teams
Why? We didn't choose one

Statement of the root cause: We didn't choose a leader or facilitator to organize planning for the enterprise

Countermeasures

Brainstorm countermeasures and evaluate each potential solution, ranking them with 5 being best and 1 being worst. You may weight-bias the categories according to company priorities.

Countermeasure	Cost	Ease to do	Control	Effectiveness (ratings of performance)	Total
Weights	0.0	0.4	0.2	0.4	
Countermeasure 1 – Appoint a leader	5	2.0	5 1.0	3 1.2	4.2
Countermeasure 2 – Group leadership	2	0.8	3 0.6	5 2.0	3.4
Countermeasure 3 – Solicit volunteer	3	1.2	2 0.4	1 0.4	2.0

Selected Countermeasure (s):

Short Term: Instructor facilitated discussion

Long Term: C/M 1 - Engage the group in a brief discussion focusing on the four current team leaders. As

Selection rationale: we learn more about the strengths of individual team leaders and team members, we will be able to decide who would make the best group leader, and ask that person to step up and take the job.

Countermeasure: Implementation Plan

Develop an implementation schedule incorporating status and results are. 0 = Acceptance; Δ = Needs improvement; x = Poor

Implementation Steps	Who's responsible	11:30	12:00	12:30	1:00	1:30	2:00	2:30	3:00	3:30	4:00	4:30	5:00	Date complete
Appoint group leader	Group		O											
Assign joint teams for problems	Group leader				O									
Present recommended C/Ms	Team leaders						O							
Implement selected C/Ms	Teams									O				
Final prep for simulation run	Teams													

Track Results

How long do we need to track results?
N/A

Number of req'd samples:
N/A

Method for tracking (visual) and location of information:
created visual info board for round 3

Confirm

Date standardized work outlined:
June 10, 2011

Document with before and after pictures for future training. Identify the location of these files for team members.

SW set held by each team leader

Standardize

Reflect

Need for more training

©2010. II.S & David Veech. All rights reserved.

C-4 Worksheet

Concern – Cause – Countermeasure – Confirm

Theme: Plywood Panel Quality
Ultimate goal: Reduce the number of shop grade panels by 20%
Date assigned: 1/17/2011

Team Member: _____ Shift: ___
Team Leader: _____ Shift: ___
C-4 Coach: _____ Shift: ___

Concern: Understand the current situation

Who discovered the problem? Gather findings from any previous studies of this problem area. Ongoing. Operators can see it when it's really bad. Patchline Operators

Describe what is happening to indicate a problem.
Panels not clearly sawed out in square. (1/2" & larger MDF & PBC). Seeing overhangs on ends and sides

Describe the ideal condition. What standard is involved if any?
Perfectly square panels with zero overhangs on panels

Use charts, diagrams or photos whenever possible to describe the situation.

Current State Value Stream or Process Map. Summarize here and indicate where others can find fully detailed map.

What are the key problem areas on the map? (What are your angry clouds?)
Overhangs
Poor cuts
Bouncing
Tails and sticks in the way

When does this problem occur? How frequently? Saw damage has occurred on 1,391 panels since Jan 1 (.31% of shop)

What is the problem costing the organization? See picture at right. Total cost $7,611 year to date.

Concern: Write your problem and goal statement

Problem: Uneven air pressure on hold down wheels
Goal: Eliminate uneven air pressure to contribute to reduction in shop panels

Cause: Analysis

Priority Causes	What else?	Who else?	When?	Evaluation	Rank order
No simple instructions	Standardized work	Operators and team leader	June 30	Which will have least cost	1
Equipment too complex	Detailed specs	Manufacturer and engineering	June 15	Which will have least cost	2

Cause: 5 Why Analysis

Problem → No simple instructions
Why? → Std Work has too many steps & small writing
Why? → Trying to capture too many functions on one set of instructions
Why? → Equipment requires many adjustments in many places
Why? → Equipment too complex

Statement of the root cause: Equipment requires many adjustments in many places

Countermeasures

Brainstorm countermeasures and evaluate each potential solution, ranking them with 5 being best and 1 being worst.

Countermeasure	Weights	Cost 0.2	Ease to do 0.2	Control 0.1	Effectiveness 0.3	Total
Countermeasure 1 – Connect to Auto setup	4	1.6	4 0.8	4 0.4	4 1.2	4.0
Countermeasure 2 – Central touch screen	3	1.2	2 0.4	3 0.3	3 0.9	2.8
Countermeasure 3 – Buy new saw	2	0.4	1 0.2	1 0.1	5 1.5	2.2
Countermeasure 4 – Standardized work	5	2.0	5 1.0	5 0.5	3 0.9	4.4

Selected Countermeasure (s):
Short Term: Enforce improved standardized work
Long Term: C/M 1 – Create and install Automatic setup. Develop new standardized work and train operators to meet the new standard.
Selection rationale:

Countermeasure: Implementation Plan

Implementation Steps	Who's responsible	2/14	2/28	3/15	3/20	4/15	4/20	5/20	6/15	6/20	7/15	7/30	Date complete
Rework current std work	Team leader	O											
Develop test panel	Maintenance/Engr		O										
Testing	CI Team/Maint/Engr			O									
Develop new std work	CI Team w/TL				O								
Final implementation of panel	CI Team/Maint/Engr					O							
All operators proficient in SW	Team leader							O					

Confirm

Date standardized work updated: April 30, 2011
How do we need to track results? Permanent inspection point
Number of reg'd samples: N/A
Method for tracking (visual) and location of information: Checked visually by operator; checked by grading system

©2010. ILS & David Veech. All rights reserved.

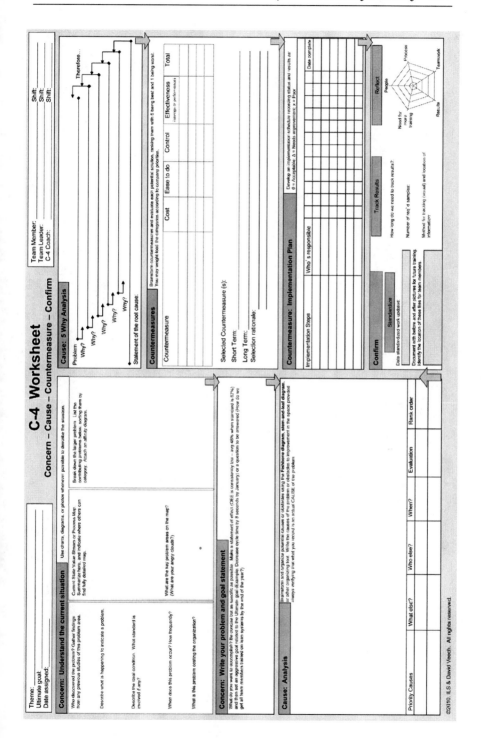

CHAPTER 7

Managing the C4 Process: Engaging Everyone

The C4 worksheet is a powerful way to initiate the C4 process within a work area, but it can be somewhat intimidating when first introduced. For problems that don't require this level of comprehensive detail, the C4 card condenses the problem-solving structure so it can be used, with coaching support, by individual employees.

Making the C4 process accessible and useful to everyone in the organization provides a channel to higher levels of employee involvement and engagement. The card gives employees a little more control over their work and their workplace. Like the C4 worksheet, the card guides employees through the problem-solving process while simultaneously building their skills in analysis, synthesis and evaluation. It's a fairly simple tool, but it still requires workers to use critical thinking to solve problems, and it does so without significant disruptions to their regular work.

Here are the four most common ways the C4 process is initiated within an organization:

1. *Alert response:* An individual employee reports a problem; the team leader or supervisor responds with a C4 card in hand.

C4 Card

Date:
Shift:
Name:
Department:
Team Leader/Supervisor:

C1-Concern: Capture the current state with a chart, picture or diagram below.

C1-Concern: Identify the problem (Who, what, when, where, how).

C2-Cause: To help identify the root cause, answer the question "Why did this happen?" Then ask why that answer happened. Do this 5 times. Write your responses here.

Cross Shift Coordination: TL/Supervisor
OK as is: _____ See note: _____

Front

C3 - Evaluate your countermeasure.
Circle the appropriate ratings.

Ease	Easy	Medium	Hard	
Cost	$	$$	$$$	?
Control	All	Some	Little	?
Effective	Yes	Maybe	No	
Savings	$$$	$$	$	?

Implementation Plan (what, who, and when):

Action steps	Who	When

C4-Confirm: Has the countermeasure been approved, implemented and standardized?

	No	Yes	Date	By whom
Approved:				
Implemented:				
Standardized:				

C3-Countermeasure: Capture the future state with a chart, picture or diagram below.

Reference #:
_____

Back

2. *Individual response:* An individual employee experiences or observes a problem, grabs a C4 card and initiates the process.

3. *Individual idea:* An individual has an idea about how to improve something in his or her work area, grabs a C4 card and initiates the process.

4. *Management response:* A manager or leader wants a team or an individual to address either a specific problem or a specific goal in a business plan and provides a C4 card to begin the process.

Beyond the first few steps, all four ways follow the same process: identify the *Concern*; find the *Cause*; develop, evaluate and implement *Countermeasures*; and *Confirm* the countermeasures were effective and the C4 process worked properly.

When using the card, the critical success factor is the specific interaction between the individual and a coach in working through the C4 process. (Sometimes, of course, this interaction may result in the employee or supervisor deciding a chartered team would be more appropriate for the problem at hand. In such a case, a problem-solving effort that began with a C4 card would migrate to a C4 worksheet.)

In the *alert response* scenario, when an individual employee experiences a problem all he has to do is report it. This approach is most appropriate for problems that threaten production (that is, if the problem isn't solved, people have to stop working). Machine breakdowns (including computers in offices); errors made by operators; accidents or safety near misses; or missing parts, information or tools are problems that could fall into this category. In organizations equipped with andon systems (systems designed to notify a succession of leaders in case of a problem), the individual employee usually needs to activate the andon system manually (by pulling a cord or pressing a button).

When a team leader or supervisor arrives in response to an

alert, the employee and leader/supervisor implement a short-term countermeasure together. They'll then grab a C4 card and document the problem, critically thinking through the *Concern*, finding the root *Cause*, and finally developing and evaluating a long-term *Countermeasure*. The most important element in this case is the response of the team leader or supervisor. If the response is not immediate, the organization risks additional costs of delay in work or, even worse, losing track of the problem as the product, report or activity continues without stopping. The C4 card serves to document the problem so the organization can keep track, spot trends and follow up to ensure long-term *Countermeasures* hold.

In the *individual response* scenario, when an employee experiences a problem he simply needs to grab a card (a supply of which should be kept near every workstation), fill in his name, and note what he thinks the problem is under C1: Concern: Identify the problem (who, what, when, where, how). This process needs to be as simple as possible to encourage everyone to use and keep using the cards. Examples like: "Bottleneck for product flow in finishing," "Paper jam in network printer 3" or "No parts in the pick bin" are fine. At this point, no other details are required. This *individual response* approach is primarily useful for problems of minor annoyance. In organizations that have used C4 for some time, it may be appropriate for an individual employee to record other, more significant problems after activating the alert system, rather than simply waiting for a team leader or supervisor to respond. This combination provides an immediate diagnosis of the problem that can help to speed the solution when a leader or supporting expert (maintenance tech, etc.) arrives to help.

The *individual idea* scenario uses the C4 card to capture employees' ideas. An employee starts the card by filling in her name and a brief description of her idea in the C3-Countermeasure section and then gives the card to her team leader or supervisor at the earliest opportunity. Once an idea has been captured, the leader or C4 coach guides the employee through the process, helping her to build skills in critical thinking, analysis and evaluation.

Usually these ideas are solutions to problems the employee has experienced in the past. The problem may not always be evident, so it's the solution that surfaces first. In other cases an idea may relate to making something in the workplace work better rather than addressing a specific problem. Ideas generated in this way are often powerful learning opportunities, since individuals typically work much harder for the success of an idea they came up with. <u>Of course, employees will only be willing to share their ideas in the first place if they feel safe doing so.</u> This is why it's so important for companies to build relationships and trust within the organization.

Most ideas generated by individual employees, like most ideas anywhere, will not be great, earth-shattering, big-money-saving game-changers. But even the worst of them helps teach individuals how to analyze and evaluate ideas. It's much better if an individual concludes through his own analysis that his idea stinks, as opposed to having someone else (a boss, a parent, an expert, a teacher) tell him it stinks.

The final scenario, *management response*, is often the <u>best place</u> to start. Almost every organization has a substantial list of valid, non-critical problems and/or goals it has compiled over a long period of time. Using the C4 card to tackle items on this list allows the organization to roll out C4 in a controlled and deliberate manner. This approach is likely to make employees more receptive to the change than simply putting a bunch of cards about the workplace and telling people to fill them out as needed.

Though not a problem per se, a goal on a business plan is an expected level of performance. And the organization is not achieving the goal, or it wouldn't be in the plan. The C4 card and C4 worksheet give managers real tools they can use to move toward their goals, rather than simply reviewing progress at a monthly meeting. To make the most effective use of these powerful tools, managers should routinely take a C4 card out into the work area and interact with employees to develop *Countermeasures* that might take them to goal-level performance.

C4 Coaching

Regardless of how a C4 card is initiated, it's the interactive learning that occurs between an employee and a leader or C4 coach that makes it so powerful. Furthermore, making this process more visible to the workforce spreads the habit, encouraging others to report and think through problems.

Once a leader secures a C4 card, his or her job is to teach individuals critical-thinking and problem-solving skills. At the first opportunity after a C4 card is initiated, the leader or C4 coach posts it on the C4 board.

> *The C4 board is a corkboard section of an integrated team information board, a central part of the management structure for a lean organization. The board provides a single place to collect and display information the team needs to ensure it's working to standardized work, achieving daily and hourly goals, developing each employee's skills, and sharing ideas and problems to drive improvement within the organization.*

The reason for this posting is two-fold: (1) It tells everyone in the area that a problem is under analysis, and (2) It keeps the problem visible, which helps to promote completion of the process.

For an *alert response,* the posting may take place after the leader and the employee have already applied a short-term countermeasure together. In the case of an *individual response* or *individual idea,* the leader may or may not have discussed the problem with the employee before posting the card. If it's a *management response,* the leader first discusses the problem with the employee and then posts the card to the board.

An example of an integrated team information board is shown on the following page.

The board is organized so cards can be tracked visually to completion. Cards are moved from column to column as key activities related to them are in process or completed. The C4 column titles are named for the steps in setting C4 as a plastic explosive, mostly to make it interesting, but also to keep titles short and simple. Each organization should feel free to create titles that work for it.

- Aimed means the coach has completed an initial discussion with the employee and the idea is waiting for input from other shifts or departments as needed.
- Armed means the leader has reported the problem or idea to the department manager and received input from others, and that the coach and employee are evaluating *Countermeasures.*
- Fire in the hole means the employee and coach have selected the best *Countermeasure* and the implementation is in process.

The card moves from New to Aimed after the leader or coach has completed an initial discussion with the employee. This discussion needs to occur on the same day the card is posted and as the employee continues working. The team leader or supervisor serves as a coach to lead the employee through the C4 process, asking leading questions about the problem and the work environment, specifically giving the employee the opportunity to practice critical thinking and problem solving.

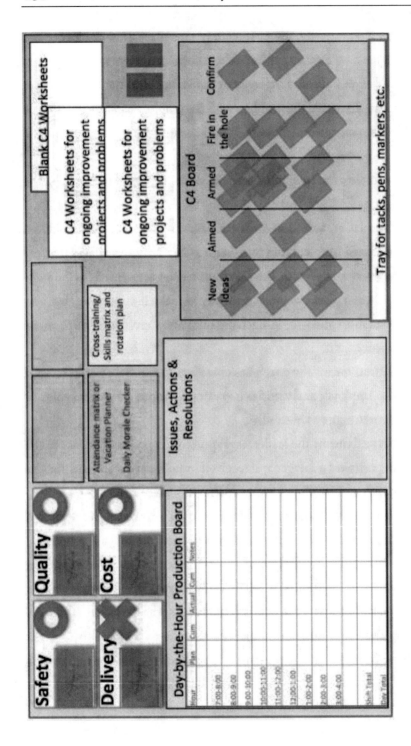

The supervisor may choose to assign the card and the task of coaching the individual employee to another employee who has been designated a C4 peer coach. C4 peer coaches have received a certain amount of training, allowing them to work with their peers in completing the C4 card.

The initial conversation should be friendly and focused on the employee. Even if the coach thinks the idea is the dumbest she's ever heard, she has to follow the process. People can learn skills related to analysis, synthesis and evaluation from dumb ideas as well as good ones. Thus it's important the coach understand her role as one of teacher rather than judge.

The coach should seek to understand the *Concern* by asking questions that make the employee think critically:

- Who discovered this problem?
- What happened, exactly?
- How often does it happen?
- Is there a pattern to when it happens (say every afternoon; or only on Wednesdays)?
- What did you do in the past when you found this problem?
- Who else has to work around this issue?
- How bad is it?

If the problem identified is substantial, the coach needs to help the employee break it down into a solvable chunk or refer it to the department manager to assemble a group or team to solve it. Leaders should insist that coaches exert considerable effort to break down problems with employees rather than refer them up the chain. A small piece of a large problem solved completely at the working level by an employee and his coach means the employee will be more willing to go through the process again. The cumulative effect of having many small problems solved is also likely to outweigh the effect of solving a single large problem over a longer period of time.

As the coach secures answers to the questions listed above, thus helping the individual more clearly define the problem, he or she writes the answers on the C4 card in the appropriate space.

Next, the coach leads the employee through a 5 whys analysis to get to the root *Cause*. This activity may require more challenging questioning to help the individual think through the causes thoroughly. A note of caution: It's very easy to fall into the trap of identifying solutions as causes. Whenever an answer reflects the absence of something (e.g., "no training" or "no standardized work" or "lack of time," etc.) it's important the coach have the employee identify the underlying problem he or she thinks the answer would solve.

Another trap easily fallen into during analysis is blaming, with the most frequently blamed entity being management. Often, individuals and groups try to work through why something has happened but get sidetracked by citing a policy or inattentive leaders as the root *Cause*. While a company policy or manager may contribute to a problem environment, leaders need to coach employees to focus on causes upon which they can take action. If the answers to the 5 whys take the problem solver outside his area of control, the leader should coach him to refocus on a path that will lead to a cause he can affect personally.

Many companies have created and use simple forms to capture employee ideas or document problems. Few of these approaches require the submitter to analyze and evaluate his own ideas or *Countermeasures*. However, to drive learning and cognitive development to the highest levels, organizations need to teach this critical skill. Like the C4 worksheet, the C4 card requires that the employee and the coach think through key elements of the proposed *Countermeasure*, evaluating its *cost, ease to do, control* and *effectiveness* as well as the savings likely to be achieved by implementing the proposed solution.

Often, an employee will need to interact with support staff to get enough information for a proper evaluation. For example, he may have to get technical estimates from engineering, financial information from accounting or materials costs from purchasing. Because the C4 process requires the employee to round up this information—with the help of the coach—the effort will require specific scheduling to ensure the employee's normal work still gets done. The organization may have to insist that support people schedule meeting times with the employee at *his* workplace rather than their own. Such a shift in focus clearly emphasizes the priority a company places on developing a problem-solving and "go and see" culture.

If an evaluated *Countermeasure* turns out to be a good one, employee and coach plan its implementation, obtain approvals or complete work orders for maintenance or engineering support, schedule the implementation and execute the schedule.

All of this may sound like a rather time-consuming process, but in the majority of cases employee, coach and supervisor are able to get through the entire process, including implementing the solution, in a single day. Imagine the impact of such execution-focused activity. Employees get positive attention and assistance when they report problems or share ideas. As more people see ideas and solutions hit their workplaces, they become more likely to report their own problems and share their own ideas. Of course, this scenario is a two-edged sword. On the one hand, the organization has a vibrant, engaged and excited workforce sharing hundreds of problems and ideas every day. On the other, the company has to make sure the best of these ideas get rapidly implemented.

The question then becomes: "Where do we get the resources to implement all these solutions?" The answer is simple. They are there already—employees, team leaders and supervisors throughout the company—working every day. The organization has only to equip them with the skills they need, then empower them to make decisions, approve action plans and obtain materials and support to solve problems effectively. Expectations of leaders must change so their first priority, the most important aspect of their job, is to teach.

The communication of problems or ideas that need higher-level support must also be fast and focused. Organizations with lean meeting structures are already positioned to include very brief problem reviews in their daily operation. C4 boards aid in this communication. As leaders make daily trips through the workplace, they'll be able to see and review the status of all C4 cards in progress.

To wrap up the process, the completed card moves to the *Confirm* column on the C4 board and the coach leads the employee through a reflection of the process, asking her to answer specific questions about the way she approached the *Concern*, *Cause* and *Countermeasure* stages, and then following up on the implemented solutions to ensure they're as effective as estimated.

Completed cards are kept on file and their contents entered into a knowledge-base so both problems and solutions are available to everyone in the organization for future reference. There are numerous ways to capture this information, but it's important to resist the temptation to automate the entire operation. The visual nature of the C4 process ensures that everyone knows the expectations and sees the status. Perhaps a designated individual could walk through the workplace, collect the completed cards from the *Confirm* columns of all C4 boards, and then enter relevant information into the knowledge-base before filing the cards.

Wrapping It Up

As a conclusion to this short book on problem solving, I wanted to take the opportunity to speak directly to you, the reader. My colleagues and I have seen remarkable changes take place in companies—large and small—that have implemented the C4 process. We know it works, and now that you've been introduced to the concept through this book you can take the first steps to make *your* firm a true learning organization. I know you can do it, but I also know how busy people tend to get. Despite the best of intentions, we've all read books and thought, *That's a cool idea; I'm going to try it.* But then life got in the way. No matter how good the idea, we didn't take the steps to put it into practice.

Fortunately, success in any transformative idea only requires that you take the first small steps, that you take action in areas where you have control, even if it's only on your desktop. Your willingness to take this action, to learn more and to share what you learn with your colleagues, is hundreds of times more important that installing new technology or hiring consultants to do the work for you.

Start with a C4 card and the person closest to you. Find a small problem and solve it together. Then try it again. As you rack up more and more solutions, you'll find others coming to you to ask how you've managed to make your part of the organization so effective.

If you ever find yourself stuck and want some feedback, send me an email to dveech@gmail.com with *C4 Help* in the subject line and I'll try to help. And good luck!

David Veech
July 2011

Index

83, 93, 103, 104, 106, 108, 113, 117, 120, 131, 132, 138, 140

Coach 2, 115, 117, 131, 133, 134, 135, 137, 138, 139, 140

Coaching viii, 134

Comprehension 21, 22

Concern vii, ix, 10, 12, 18, 25, 26, 27, 28, 29, 31, 33, 34, 35, 37, 39, 41, 43, 45, 47, 49, 50, 51, 52, 53, 54, 55, 56, 57, 59, 60, 61, 62, 63, 64, 67, 68, 69, 70, 77, 78, 83, 87, 88, 91, 93, 103, 113, 117, 118, 119, 120, 131, 132, 137, 140

Concern-Cause-Countermeasure ix

Confidence (see also Self-efficacy) 23, 115, 119

Confirm viii, ix, 10, 11, 26, 112, 113, 115, 117, 118, 119, 120, 121, 123, 125, 127, 131, 140

Contain viii, 83

Countermeasure viii, ix, 10, 11, 26, 27, 61, 83, 84, 85, 86, 87, 88, 89, 90, 91, 93, 94, 95, 96, 97, 98, 99, 100, 101, 103, 104, 105, 107, 109, 110, 111, 113, 117, 119, 120, 122, 123, 132, 135, 138, 139, 140

Critical Thinking vii, 23, 25, 27, 28, 29, 31, 33, 35, 37, 39, 41, 43, 45, 47, 49, 51, 53, 55, 57, 59, 70, 86, 94, 117, 129, 133, 135

Culture 8, 21, 114, 115, 139

D

Data 10, 11, 26, 31, 32, 33, 36, 37, 48, 51, 54, 55, 57, 60, 64, 65, 70, 72, 87, 88, 91, 94, 98, 100, 121

Decision Matrix viii, 17, 95, 97, 100, 105, 110

Discipline 7, 8, 18, 23, 64, 114

E

Evaluate viii, 83, 94

Evaluation 8, 11, 21, 22, 23, 55, 87, 88, 89, 90, 92, 93, 94, 97, 98, 99, 100, 102, 103, 104, 107, 108, 110, 129, 133, 137, 139

Evaluation Criteria viii, 87, 97, 99

F

Fishbone Cause-and-Effect viii, 67

Fishbone diagram x, 67, 70, 74

Formulate viii, 7, 10, 83, 87, 93

I

Ideas 11, 12, 18, 19, 20, 23, 93, 94, 104, 115, 116, 124, 132, 133, 134, 137, 138, 139, 140

Implement viii, 10, 11, 12, 16, 27, 30, 83, 87, 90, 91, 99, 100, 102, 104, 105, 108, 110, 111, 123, 131, 132, 139

Individual idea 131, 132, 135

Individual response 132, 135

K

Kaizen x, 12, 17

Knowledge 9, 21, 22, 34, 140

L

Learning vii, viii, ix, x, 1, 8, 9, 10, 21, 22, 23, 29, 30, 65, 102, 113, 115, 116, 117, 118, 119, 120, 121, 123, 125, 127, 133, 134, 138, 141

M

Management response 133, 135

Measurement 68, 88, 98, 118

Metrics 33, 118

Multi-voting vii, 16, 48, 49, 50, 51, 60, 94

P

PDCA 9

Plan viii, ix, 2, 9, 10, 11, 46, 68, 83, 90, 96, 101, 102, 103, 111, 123, 131, 133, 134, 139

Plan-Do-Check-Act 9

Problem vii, 2, 3, 4, 5, 7, 8, 9, 10, 11, 12, 15, 17, 18, 19, 20, 21, 22, 25, 26, 27, 28, 29, 30, 31, 32, 33, 34, 35, 36, 37, 40, 41, 42, 44, 45, 46, 47, 48, 49, 50, 51, 52, 53, 56, 57, 59, 60, 61, 62, 63, 64, 65, 66, 67, 68, 69, 70, 72, 73, 75, 77, 78, 80, 81, 82, 83, 84, 85, 86, 87, 92, 93, 94, 102, 103, 104, 106, 107, 113, 115, 119, 120, 122, 123, 124, 129, 131, 132, 133, 134, 135, 137, 138, 139, 140, 141, 142

Problem solving 4, 9, 10, 11, 18, 21, 29, 61, 77, 102, 122, 124, 135, 141

Problem Statement vii, 51, 52, 60, 67, 68

Q

Quality Circle 15, 16, 17, 28

R

Reflect viii, 3, 10, 38, 113, 120, 121, 123

S

Self-efficacy (see also Confidence) 23, 114, 115, 117

Simulation vii, 29, 30, 31, 55, 77, 91, 103, 104, 106, 122

Standardize viii, 10, 113, 114, 117

Standardized work 10, 67, 74, 81, 107, 109, 110, 111, 114, 115, 116, 117, 119, 122, 123, 134, 138

Stem-and-Leaf Cause Analysis viii, 70

StrikeFighter vii, viii, 29, 34, 40, 42, 50, 51, 55, 62, 70, 77, 78, 103, 107, 122

Structured brainstorming 19, 20, 42, 93

Synthesis 8, 21, 22, 23, 129, 137

T

Team 2, 4, 11, 13, 15, 16, 17, 18, 19, 20, 26, 27, 30, 41, 43, 46, 47, 48, 49, 50, 51, 52, 53, 56, 57, 59, 60, 63, 64, 67, 77, 78, 80, 81, 85, 87, 90, 91, 93, 94, 100, 101, 102, 103, 104, 105, 106, 108, 110, 111, 112, 115, 116, 119, 120, 121, 122, 123, 124, 129, 131, 132, 133, 134, 135, 137, 139

Track Results viii, 118

U

Unstructured brainstorming 19, 20, 68, 93

W

Waste viii, 27, 41, 42

CPSIA information can be obtained at www.ICGtesting.com
Printed in the USA
BVOW03s2344021114

373216BV00010B/175/P

9 780983 263951